गणेश पूजा

Gaṇeśa Pūjā

by
Swami Satyananda Saraswati

by Devi Mandir Publications
5950 Highway 128
Napa, CA 94558 USA
Communications: Phone and Fax 1-707-966-2802
E-Mail swamiji@shreemaa.org
Please visit us on the World Wide Web at
http://www.shreemaa.org

ISBN 1-877795-46-1
Library of Congress Catalog Card Number
CIP 2001 126529

Gaṇeśa Pūjā
Swami Satyananda Saraswati
1. Hindu Religion. 2. Worship. 3. Spirituality.
4. Philosophy. I. Saraswati, Swami Satyananda.

देवता प्रणाम्

devatā praṇām

श्रीमन्महागणाधिपतये नमः

śrīmanmahāgaṇādhipataye namaḥ

We bow to the Respected Great Lord of Wisdom.

लक्ष्मीनारायणाभ्यां नमः

lakṣmīnārāyaṇābhyāṃ namaḥ

We bow to Lakṣmī and Nārāyaṇa, The Goal of all Existence and the Perceiver of all.

उमामहेश्वराभ्यां नमः

umāmaheśvarābhyāṃ namaḥ

We bow to Umā and Maheśvara, She who protects existence, and the Great Consciousness or Seer of all.

वाणीहिरण्यगर्भाभ्यां नमः

vāṇīhiraṇyagarbhābhyāṃ namaḥ

We bow to Vāṇī and Hiraṇyagarbha, Sarasvatī and Brahmā, who create the cosmic existence.

शचीपुरन्दराभ्यां नमः

śacīpurandarābhyāṃ namaḥ

We bow to Śacī and Purandara, Indra and his wife, who preside over all that is divine.

मातापितृभ्यां नमः

mātāpitṛbhyāṃ namaḥ

We bow to the Mothers and Fathers.

इष्टदेवताभ्यो नमः

iṣṭadevatābhyo namaḥ
We bow to the chosen deity of worship.

कुलदेवताभ्यो नमः

kuladevatābhyo namaḥ
We bow to the family deity of worship.

ग्रामदेवताभ्यो नमः

grāmadevatābhyo namaḥ
We bow to the village deity of worship.

वास्तुदेवताभ्यो नमः

vāstudevatābhyo namaḥ
We bow to the particular household deity of worship.

स्थानदेवताभ्यो नमः

sthānadevatābhyo namaḥ
We bow to the established deity of worship.

सर्वेभ्यो देवेभ्यो नमः

sarvebhyo devebhyo namaḥ
We bow to all the Gods.

सर्वेभ्यो ब्राह्मणेभ्यो नमः

sarvebhyo brāhmaṇebhyo namaḥ
We bow to all the Knowers of divinity.

Gaṇeśa Pūjā

(Wave light)

ॐ अग्निर्ज्योती रविर्ज्योतिश्चन्द्रो ज्योतिस्तथैव च ।

ज्योतिषामुत्तमो देव दीपोऽयं प्रतिगृह्यताम् ॥

एष दीपः ॐ गं गणपतये नमः ॥

oṃ agnirjyotī ravirjyotiścandro jyotistathaiva ca
jyotiṣāmuttamo deva dīpo-yaṃ pratigṛhyatām
eṣa dīpaḥ oṃ gaṃ gaṇapataye namaḥ

oṃ The Divine Fire is the Light, the Light of Wisdom is the Light, the Light of Devotion is the Light as well. The Light of the Highest Bliss, Oh God, is in the Light which we offer, the Light which we request you to accept. With the offering of Light, Oṃ we bow to the Lord of Wisdom, Lord of the Multitudes.

(Wave incense)

ॐ वनस्पतिरसोत्पन्नो गन्धात्ययी गन्ध उत्तमः ।

आघ्रेयः सर्वदेवानां धूपोऽयं प्रतिगृह्यताम् ॥

एष धूपः ॐ गं गणपतये नमः ॥

oṃ vanaspatirasotpanno gandhātyayī gandha uttamaḥ
āghreyaḥ sarvadevānāṃ dhūpo-yaṃ pratigṛhyatām
eṣa dhūpaḥ oṃ gaṃ gaṇapataye namaḥ

oṃ Spirit of the Forest, from you is produced the most excellent of scents. The scent most pleasing to all the Gods, that scent we request you to accept. With the offering of fragrant scent, Oṃ we bow to the Lord of Wisdom, Lord of the Multitudes.

ārātrikam

ॐ चन्द्रादित्यौ च धरणी विद्युदग्निस्तथैव च ।

त्वमेव सर्वज्योतीषिं आरात्रिकं प्रतिगृह्यताम् ॥

ॐ गं गणपतये नमः आरात्रिकं समर्पयामि

oṃ candrādityau ca dharaṇī
vidyudagnistathaiva ca
tvameva sarvajyotīṣiṃ ārātrikaṃ pratigṛhyatām
oṃ gaṃ gaṇapataye namaḥ ārātrikaṃ samarpayāmi

All knowing as the Moon, the Sun and the Divine Fire, you alone are all light, and this light we request you to accept. With the offering of light, Oṃ we bow to the Lord of Wisdom, Lord of the Multitudes.

ॐ पयः पृथिव्यां पय ओषधीषु

पयो दिव्यन्तरिक्षे पयो धाः ।

पयःस्वतीः प्रदिशः सन्तु मह्यम् ॥

oṃ payaḥ pṛthivyāṃ paya oṣadhīṣu
payo divyantarikṣe payo dhāḥ
payaḥsvatīḥ pradiśaḥ santu mahyam

oṃ Earth is a reservoir of nectar, all vegetation is a reservoir of nectar, the divine atmosphere is a reservoir of nectar, and also above. May all perceptions shine forth with the sweet taste of nectar for us.

ॐ अग्निर्देवता वातो देवता सूर्यो देवता चन्द्रमा देवता वसवो

देवता रुद्रो देवता ऽदित्या देवता मरुतो देवता विश्वे देवा देवता

बृहस्पतिर्देवतेन्द्रो देवता वरुणो देवता ॥

oṃ agnirdevatā vāto devatā sūryo devatā candramā devatā vasavo devatā rudro devatā-dityā devatā maruto devatā viśve devā devatā bṛhaspatirdevatendro devatā varuṇo devatā

oṃ The Divine Fire (Light of Purity) is the shining God, the Wind is the shining God, the Sun (Light of Wisdom) is the shining God, the Moon (Lord of Devotion) is the shining God, the Protectors of the Wealth are the shining Gods, the Relievers of Sufferings are the shining Gods, the Sons of the Light are the shining Gods; the Emancipated seers (Maruts) are the shining Gods, the Universal Shining Gods are the shining Gods, the Guru of the Gods is the shining God, the Ruler of the Gods is the shining God, the Lord of Waters is the shining God.

ॐ भूर्भुवः स्वः ।

तत् सवितुर्वरेण्यम् भर्गो देवस्य धीमहि ।

धियो यो नः प्रचोदयात् ॥

oṃ bhūr bhuvaḥ svaḥ
tat savitur vareṇyam bhargo devasya dhīmahi
dhiyo yo naḥ pracodayāt

oṃ the Infinite Beyond Conception, the gross body, the subtle body and the causal body; we meditate upon that Light of Wisdom which is the Supreme Wealth of the Gods. May it grant to us increase in our meditations.

ॐ भूः

oṃ bhūḥ
oṃ the gross body

ॐ भुवः

oṃ bhuvaḥ
oṃ the subtle body

ॐ स्वः

oṃ svaḥ
oṃ the causal body

ॐ महः

oṃ mahaḥ
oṃ the great body of existence

ॐ जनः

oṃ janaḥ
oṃ the body of knowledge

ॐ तपः

oṃ tapaḥ
oṃ the body of light

ॐ सत्यं

oṃ satyaṃ
oṃ the body of Truth

ॐ तत् सवितुर्वरेण्यम् भर्गो देवस्य धीमहि ।

धियो यो नः प्रचोदयात् ॥

oṃ tat savitur vareṇyam bhargo devasya dhīmahi
dhiyo yo naḥ pracodayāt

oṃ we meditate upon that Light of Wisdom which is the Supreme Wealth of the Gods. May it grant to us increase in our meditations.

ॐ आपो ज्योतीरसोमृतं ब्रह्म भूर्भुवस्स्वरोम् ॥

oṃ āpo jyotīrasomṛtaṃ brahma bhūrbhuvassvarom

May the divine waters luminous with the nectar of immortality of Supreme Divinity fill the earth, the atmosphere and the heavens.

ॐ मां माले महामाये सर्वशक्तिस्वरूपिणि ।

चतुर्वर्गस्त्वयि न्यस्तस्तस्मान्मे सिद्धिदा भव ॥

oṃ māṃ māle mahāmāye sarvaśaktisvarūpiṇi
catur vargas tvayi nyastas tasmān me siddhidā bhava

oṃ My Rosary, The Great Measurement of Consciousness, containing all energy within as your intrinsic nature, give to me the attainment of your Perfection, fulfilling the four objectives of life.

ॐ अविघ्नं कुरु माले त्वं गृह्णामि दक्षिणे करे ।

जपकाले च सिद्ध्यर्थं प्रसीद मम सिद्धये ॥

oṃ avighnaṃ kuru māle tvaṃ
gṛhṇāmi dakṣiṇe kare
japakāle ca siddhyarthaṃ prasīda mama siddhaye

oṃ Rosary, You please remove all obstacles. I hold you in my right hand. At the time of recitation be pleased with me. Allow me to attain the Highest Perfection.

ॐ अक्षमालाधिपतये सुसिद्धिं देहि देहि सर्वमन्त्रार्थसाधिनि साधय साधय सर्वसिद्धिं परिकल्पय परिकल्पय मे स्वाहा ॥

oṃ akṣa mālā dhipataye susiddhiṃ dehi dehi sarva mantrārtha sādhini sādhaya sādhaya sarva siddhiṃ parikalpaya parikalpaya me svāhā

oṃ Rosary of rudrākṣa seeds, my Lord, give to me excellent attainment. Give to me, give to me. Illuminate the meanings of all mantras, illuminate, illuminate! Fashion me with all excellent attainments, fashion me! I am One with God!

एते गन्धपुष्पे ॐ गं गणपतये नमः

ete gandhapuṣpe oṃ gaṃ gaṇapataye namaḥ

With these scented flowers oṃ we bow to the Lord of Wisdom, Lord of the Multitudes.

एते गन्धपुष्पे ॐ आदित्यादिनवग्रहेभ्यो नमः

ete gandhapuṣpe oṃ ādityādi navagrahebhyo namaḥ

With these scented flowers oṃ we bow to the Sun, the Light of Wisdom, along with the nine planets.

एते गन्धपुष्पे ॐ शिवादिपञ्चदेवताभ्यो नमः

ete gandhapuṣpe oṃ śivādipañcadevatābhyo namaḥ

With these scented flowers oṃ we bow to Śiva, the Consciousness of Infinite Goodness, along with the five primary deities (Śiva, Śakti, Viṣṇu, Gaṇeśa, Sūrya).

एते गन्धपुष्पे ॐ इन्द्रादिदशदिक्पालेभ्यो नमः

ete gandhapuṣpe oṃ indrādi daśadikpālebhyo namaḥ

With these scented flowers oṃ we bow to Indra, the Ruler of the Pure, along with the Ten Protectors of the ten directions.

एते गन्धपुष्पे ॐ मत्स्यादिदशावतारेभ्यो नमः

ete gandhapuṣpe oṃ matsyādi daśāvatārebhyo namaḥ

With these scented flowers oṃ we bow to Viṣṇu, the Fish, along with the Ten Incarnations which He assumed.

एते गन्धपुष्पे ॐ प्रजापतये नमः

ete gandhapuṣpe oṃ prajāpataye namaḥ

With these scented flowers oṃ we bow to the Lord of All Created Beings.

एते गन्धपुष्पे ॐ नमो नारायणाय नमः

ete gandhapuṣpe oṃ namo nārāyaṇāya namaḥ

With these scented flowers oṃ we bow to the Perfect Perception of Consciousness.

एते गन्धपुष्पे ॐ सर्वेभ्यो देवेभ्यो नमः

ete gandhapuṣpe oṃ sarvebhyo devebhyo namaḥ

With these scented flowers oṃ we bow to All the Gods.

एते गन्धपुष्पे ॐ सर्वाभ्यो देवीभ्यो नमः

ete gandhapuṣpe oṃ sarvābhyo devībhyo namaḥ

With these scented flowers oṃ we bow to All the Goddesses.

एते गन्धपुष्पे ॐ श्री गुरवे नमः

ete gandhapuṣpe oṃ śrī gurave namaḥ

With these scented flowers oṃ we bow to the Guru.

एते गन्धपुष्पे ॐ ब्राह्मणेभ्यो नमः

ete gandhapuṣpe oṃ brāhmaṇebhyo namaḥ

With these scented flowers oṃ we bow to All Knowers of Wisdom.

Tie a piece of string around right middle finger or wrist.

ॐ कुशासने स्थितो ब्रह्मा कुशे चैव जनार्दनः ।

कुशे ह्याकाशवद् विष्णुः कुशासन नमोऽस्तु ते ॥

oṃ kuśāsane sthito brahmā kuśe caiva janārdanaḥ
kuśe hyākāśavad viṣṇuḥ kuśāsana namo-stu te

Brahmā is in the shining light (or kuśa grass), in the shining light resides Janārdana, the Lord of Beings. The Supreme all-pervading Consciousness, Viṣṇu, resides in the shining light. Oh Repository of the shining light, we bow down to you, the seat of kuśa grass.

आचमन

ācamana

ॐ केशवाय नमः स्वाहा

oṃ keśavāya namaḥ svāhā

We bow to the one of beautiful hair.

ॐ माधवाय नमः स्वाहा

oṃ mādhavāya namaḥ svāhā

We bow to the one who is always sweet.

ॐ गोविन्दाय नमः स्वाहा

oṃ govindāya namaḥ svāhā

We bow to He who is one-pointed light.

ॐ विष्णुः ॐ विष्णुः ॐ विष्णुः

oṃ viṣṇuḥ oṃ viṣṇuḥ oṃ viṣṇuḥ

oṃ Consciousness, oṃ Consciousness, oṃ Consciousness.

ॐ तत् विष्णोः परमं पदम् सदा पश्यन्ति सूरयः ।

दिवीव चक्षुराततम् ॥

oṃ tat viṣṇoḥ paramaṃ padam sadā paśyanti sūrayaḥ
divīva cakṣurā tatam

oṃ That Consciousness of the highest station, who always sees the Light of Wisdom, give us Divine Eyes.

ॐ तद् विप्र स पिपानोव जुविग्रन्सो सोमिन्द्रते ।

विष्णुः तत् परमं पदम् ॥

oṃ tad vipra sa pipānova juvigranso somindrate
viṣṇuḥ tat paramaṃ padam

oṃ That twice-born teacher who is always thirsty for accepting the nectar of devotion, Oh Consciousness, you are in that highest station.

ॐ अपवित्रः पवित्रो वा सर्वावस्थां गतोऽपि वा ।

यः स्मरेत् पुण्डरीकाक्षं स बाह्याभ्यन्तरः शुचिः ॥

oṃ apavitraḥ pavitro vā sarvāvasthāṃ gato-pi vā
yaḥ smaret puṇḍarīkākṣaṃ sa bāhyābhyantaraḥ śuciḥ

oṃ The Impure and the Pure reside within all objects. Who remembers the lotus-eyed Consciousness is conveyed to radiant beauty.

ॐ सर्वमङ्गलमाङ्गल्यम् वरेण्यम् वरदं शुभं ।

नारायणं नमस्कृत्य सर्वकर्माणि कारयेत् ॥

oṃ sarva maṅgala māṅgalyam
vareṇyam varadaṃ śubhaṃ
nārāyaṇaṃ namaskṛtya sarvakarmāṇi kārayet

All the Welfare of all Welfare, the highest blessing of Purity and

Illumination, with the offering of respect we bow down to the Supreme Consciousness who is the actual performer of all action.

ॐ सूर्य्यश्चमेति मन्त्रस्य ब्रह्मा ऋषिः प्रकृतिश्छन्दः आपो देवता आचमने विनियोगः ॥

oṃ sūryyaścameti mantrasya brahmā ṛṣiḥ prakṛtiśchandaḥ āpo devatā ācamane viniyogaḥ

oṃ these are the mantras of the Light of Wisdom, the Creative Capacity is the Seer, Nature is the meter, the divine flow of waters is the deity, being applied in washing the hands and rinsing the mouth.

Draw the following yantra with some drops of water and/or sandal paste at the front of your seat.

Place a flower on the bindu in the middle.

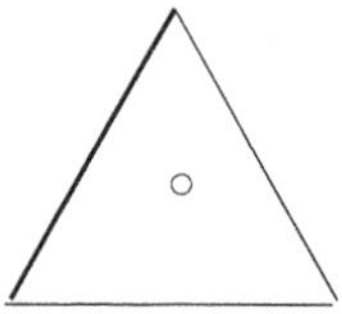

ॐ आसनस्य मन्त्रस्य मेरुपृष्ठ ऋषिः सुतलं छन्दः कूर्म्मो देवता आसनोपवेशने विनियोगः ॥

oṃ āsanasya mantrasya merupṛṣṭha ṛṣiḥ sutalaṃ chandaḥ kūrmmo devatā āsanopaveśane viniyogaḥ

Introducing the mantras of the Purification of the seat. The Seer is He whose back is Straight, the meter is of very beautiful form, the tortoise who supports the earth is the deity. These mantras are applied to make the seat free from obstructions.

एते गन्धपुष्पे ॐ ह्रीं आधारशक्तये कमलासनाय नमः ॥

ete gandhapuṣpe oṃ hrīṃ ādhāraśaktaye kamalāsanāya namaḥ

With these scented flowers oṃ hrīṃ we bow to the Primal Energy situated in this lotus seat.

ॐ पृथ्वि त्वया धृता लोका देवि त्वं विष्णुना धृता ।

त्वञ्च धारय मां नित्यं पवित्रं कुरु चासनम् ॥

oṃ pṛthvi tvayā dhṛtā lokā devi tvaṃ viṣṇunā dhṛtā
tvañca dhāraya māṃ nityaṃ pavitraṃ kuru cāsanam

oṃ Earth! You support the realms of the Goddess. You are supported by the Supreme Consciousness. Also bear me eternally and make pure this seat.

ॐ गुरुभ्यो नमः

oṃ gurubhyo namaḥ

oṃ I bow to the Guru.

ॐ परमगुरुभ्यो नमः

oṃ paramagurubhyo namaḥ

oṃ I bow to the Guru's Guru.

ॐ परापरगुरुभ्यो नमः

oṃ parāparagurubhyo namaḥ

oṃ I bow to the Gurus of the lineage.

ॐ परमेष्ठिगुरुभ्यो नमः

oṃ parameṣṭhigurubhyo namaḥ

oṃ I bow to the Supreme Gurus.

ॐ गं गणेशाय नमः

oṃ gaṃ gaṇeśāya namaḥ

oṃ I bow to the Lord of Wisdom.

ॐ अनन्ताय नमः

oṃ anantāya namaḥ
oṃ I bow to the Infinite One.

ॐ ऐं ह्रीं क्लीं चामुण्डायै विच्चे

oṃ aiṃ hrīṃ klīṃ cāmuṇḍāyai vicce
oṃ Creation, Circumstance, Transformation are known by Consciousness.

ॐ नमः शिवाय

oṃ namaḥ śivāya
oṃ I bow to the Consciousness of Infinite Goodness.

Clap hands 3 times and snap fingers in the ten directions
(N S E W NE SW NW SE UP DOWN) repeating

ॐ गं गणपतये नमः

oṃ gaṃ gaṇapataye namaḥ
oṃ we bow to the Lord of Wisdom, Lord of the Multitudes.

सङ्कल्प

saṅkalpa

विष्णुः ॐ तत् सत् । ॐ अद्य जम्बूद्वीपे ( ) देशे ( ) प्रदेशे ( ) नगरे ( ) मन्दिरे ( ) मासे ( ) पक्षे ( ) तिथौ ( ) गोत्र श्री ( ) कृतैतत् श्रीगणेशकामः पूजाकर्माहं श्रीगणेशपूजां करिष्ये ॥

viṣṇuḥ oṃ tat sat oṃ adya jambūdvīpe (Country) deśe (State) pradeśe (City) nagare (Name of house or temple) mandire (month) māse (śukla or kṛṣṇa) pakṣe (name of day) tithau (name of) gotra śrī (your name) kṛtaitat śrī gaṇeśa kāmaḥ pūjā karmāhaṃ śrī gaṇeśa pūjāṃ kariṣye

The Consciousness Which Pervades All, oṃ That is Truth. Presently, on the Planet Earth, Country of (Name), State of (Name), City of (Name), in the Temple of (Name), (Name of Month) Month, (Bright or Dark) fortnight, (Name of Day) Day, (Name of Sādhu Family), Śrī (Your Name) is performing the worship for the satisfaction of Gaṇeśa by reciting the Gaṇeśa Worship.

ॐ यज्जाग्रतो दूरमुदेति दैवं तदु सुप्तस्य तथैवैति ।
दूरङ्गमं ज्योतिषां ज्योतिरेकं तन्मे मनः शिवसङ्कल्पमस्तु ॥

oṃ yajjāgrato dūramudeti daivaṃ
tadu suptasya tathaivaiti
dūraṅgamaṃ jyotiṣāṃ jyotirekaṃ
tanme manaḥ śiva saṅkalpamastu

Oṃ May our waking consciousness replace pain and suffering with divinity as also our awareness when asleep. Far extending be our radiant aura of light, filling our minds with light. May that be the firm determination of the Consciousness of Infinite Goodness.

या गुङ्गूर्या सिनीवाली या राका या सरस्वती ।
ईन्द्राणीमह्व ऊतये वरुणानीं स्वस्तये ॥

yā guṅgūryā sinīvālī yā rākā yā sarasvatī
īndrāṇīmahva ūtaye varuṇānīṃ svastaye

May that Goddess who wears the Moon of Devotion protect the children of Devotion. May that Goddess of All-Pervading Knowledge protect us. May the Energy of the Rule of the Pure rise up. Oh Energy of Equilibrium grant us the highest prosperity.

ॐ स्वस्ति न इन्द्रो वृद्धश्रवाः स्वस्ति नः पूषा विश्ववेदाः ।
स्वस्ति नस्तार्क्ष्यो अरिष्टनेमिः स्वस्ति नो बृहस्पतिर्दधातु ॥

oṃ svasti na indro vṛddhaśravāḥ
svasti naḥ pūṣā viśvavedāḥ
svasti nastārkṣyo ariṣṭanemiḥ
svasti no bṛhaspatirdadhātu

Oṃ The Ultimate Prosperity to us, Oh Rule of the Pure, who perceives all that changes; the Ultimate Prosperity to us, Searchers for Truth, Knowers of the Universe; the Ultimate Prosperity to us, Oh Divine Being of Light, keep us safe; the Ultimate Prosperity to us, Oh Spirit of All-Pervading Delight, grant that to us.

ॐ गणानां त्वा गणपति९ हवामहे

प्रियाणां त्वा प्रियपति९ हवामहे

निधीनां त्वा निधिपति९ हवामहे वसो मम ।

आहमजानि गर्ब्भधमा त्वमजासि गर्ब्भधम् ॥

oṃ gaṇānāṃ tvā gaṇapati guṃ havāmahe
priyāṇāṃ tvā priyapati guṃ havāmahe
nidhīnāṃ tvā nidhipati guṃ havāmahe vaso mama
āhamajāni garbbhadhamā tvamajāsi garbbhadham

Oṃ We invoke you with offerings, Oh Lord of the Multitudes; we invoke you with offerings, Oh Lord of Love; we invoke you with offerings, Oh Guardian of the Treasure. Sit within me, giving birth to the realm of the Gods within me; yes, giving birth to the realm of the Gods within me.

ॐ गणानां त्वा गणपति९ हवामहे

कविं कवीनामुपमश्रवस्तमम् ।

ज्येष्ठराजं ब्रह्मणां ब्रह्मणस्पत

आ नः शृण्वन्नूतिभिः सीद सादनम् ॥

oṃ gaṇānāṃ tvā gaṇapati guṃ havāmahe
kaviṃ kavīnāmupamaśravastamam
jyeṣṭharājaṃ brahmaṇāṃ brahmaṇaspata
ā naḥ śṛnvannūtibhiḥ sīda sādanam

Oṃ We invoke you with offerings, Oh Lord of the Multitudes, Seer among Seers, of unspeakable grandeur. Oh Glorious King, Lord of the Knowers of Wisdom, come speedily hearing our supplications and graciously take your seat amidst our assembly.

ॐ अदितिर्द्यौरदितिरन्तरिक्षमदितिर्माता स पिता स पुत्रः ।
विश्वे देवा अदितिः पञ्च जना अदितिर्जातमदितिर्जनित्वम् ॥

oṃ aditir dyauraditirantarikṣamaditirmātā
sa pitā sa putraḥ
viśve devā aditiḥ pañca janā
aditirjātamaditirjanitvam

Oṃ The Mother of Enlightenment pervades the heavens; the Mother of Enlightenment pervades the atmosphere; the Mother of Enlightenment pervades Mother and Father and child. All Gods of the Universe are pervaded by the Mother, the five forms of living beings, all Life. The Mother of Enlightenment, She is to be known.

ॐ त्वं स्त्रीस्त्वं पुमानसि त्वं कुमार अत वा कुमारी ।
त्वं जिर्नो दण्डेन वञ्चसि त्वं जातो भवसि विश्वतोमुखः ॥

oṃ tvaṃ strīstvaṃ pumānasi
tvaṃ kumāra ata vā kumarī
tvaṃ jirno daṇḍena vañcasi
tvaṃ jāto bhavasi viśvatomukhaḥ

Oṃ You are Female, you are Male; you are a young boy, you are a young girl. You are the word of praise by which we are singing; you are all creation existing as the mouth of the universe.

ॐ अम्बेऽम्बिकेऽम्बालिके न मा नयति कश्चन ।

ससस्त्यश्वकः सुभद्रिकां काम्पीलवासिनीम् ॥

oṃ ambe-mbike-mbālike na mā nayati kaścana
sasastyaśvakaḥ subhadrikāṃ kāmpīlavāsinīm

Oṃ Mother of the Perceivable Universe, Mother of the Conceivable Universe, Mother of the Universe of Intuitive Vision, lead me to that True Existence. As excellent crops (or grains) are harvested, so may I be taken to reside with the Infinite Consciousness.

ॐ शान्ता द्यौः शान्तापृथिवी शान्तमिदमुर्वन्तरिक्षम् ।

शान्ता उदन्वतिरापः शान्ताः नः शान्त्वोषधीः ॥

oṃ śāntā dyauḥ śāntā pṛthivī śāntam idamurvantarikṣam
śāntā udanvatirāpaḥ śāntāḥ naḥ śāntvoṣadhīḥ

Oṃ Peace in the heavens, Peace on the earth, Peace upwards and permeating the atmosphere; Peace upwards, over, on all sides and further; Peace to us, Peace to all vegetation;

ॐ शान्तानि पूर्वरूपाणि शान्तं नोऽस्तु कृताकृतम् ।

शान्तं भूतं च भव्यं च सर्वमेव शमस्तु नः ॥

oṃ śāntāni pūrva rūpāṇi śāntaṃ no-stu kṛtākṛtam
śāntaṃ bhūtaṃ ca bhavyaṃ ca sarvameva śamastu naḥ

Oṃ Peace to all that has form, Peace to all causes and effects; Peace to all existence, and to all intensities of reality including all and everything; Peace be to us.

ॐ पृथिवी शान्तिरन्तरिक्षं शान्तिर्द्यौः

शान्तिरापः शान्तिरोषधयः शान्तिः वनस्पतयः शान्तिर्विश्वे मे

देवाः शान्तिः सर्वे मे देवाः शान्तिर्ब्रह्म शान्तिरापः शान्तिः सर्वं

शान्तिरेधि शान्तिः शान्तिः सर्व शान्तिः सा मा शान्तिः

शान्तिभिः ॥

oṃ pṛthivī śāntir antarikṣaṃ śāntir dyauḥ śāntir āpaḥ śāntir oṣadhayaḥ śāntiḥ vanaspatayaḥ śāntir viśve me devāḥ śāntiḥ sarve me devāḥ śāntir brahma śāntirāpaḥ śāntiḥ sarvaṃ śāntiredhi śāntiḥ śāntiḥ sarva śāntiḥ sā mā śāntiḥ śāntibhiḥ

Oṃ Let the earth be at Peace, the atmosphere be at Peace, the heavens be filled with Peace. Even further may Peace extend, Peace be to waters, Peace to all vegetation, Peace to All Gods of the Universe, Peace to All Gods within us, Peace to Creative Consciousness, Peace be to Brilliant Light, Peace to All, Peace to Everything, Peace, Peace, altogether Peace, equally Peace, by means of Peace.

ताभिः शान्तिभिः सर्वशान्तिभिः समया मोहं यदिह घोरं यदिह

क्रूरं यदिह पापं तच्छान्तं तच्छिवं सर्वमेव समस्तु नः ॥

tābhiḥ śāntibhiḥ sarva śāntibhiḥ samayā mohaṃ yadiha ghoraṃ yadiha krūraṃ yadiha pāpaṃ tacchāntaṃ tacchivaṃ sarvameva samastu naḥ

Thus by means of Peace, altogether one with the means of Peace, Ignorance is eliminated, Violence is eradicated, Improper Conduct is eradicated, Confusion (sin) is eradicated, all that is, is at Peace, all that is perceived, each and everything, altogether for us,

Gaṇeśa Pūjā

ॐ शान्तिः शान्तिः शान्तिः ॥

oṃ śāntiḥ śāntiḥ śāntiḥ

oṃ Peace, Peace, Peace

Draw the following yantra on the plate or space for worship with sandal paste and/or water. Offer rice on the yantra for each of the next four mantras.

ॐ आधारशक्तये नमः

oṃ ādhāra śaktaye namaḥ

oṃ I bow to the Primal Energy

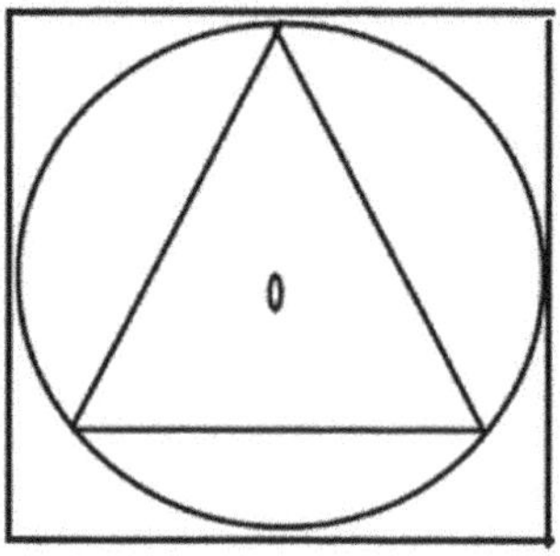

ॐ कुर्म्माय नमः

oṃ kurmmāya namaḥ

oṃ I bow to the Support of the Earth

ॐ अनन्ताय नमः

oṃ anantāya namaḥ

oṃ I bow to Infinity

ॐ पृथिव्यै नमः

oṃ pṛthivyai namaḥ

oṃ I bow to the Earth

Place an empty water pot on the bindu in the center of the yantra when saying **phaṭ**

स्थां स्थीं स्थीरो भव फट्

sthāṃ sthīṃ sthīro bhava phaṭ

Be Still in the Gross Body! Be Still in the Subtle Body! Be Still in the Causal Body! PURIFY!

Gaṇeśa Pūjā

Fill pot with water while chanting mantra.

ॐ गङ्गे च यमुने चैव गोदावरि सरस्वति ।

नर्मदे सिन्धुकावेरि जलेऽस्मिन् सन्निधिं कुरु ॥

oṃ gaṅge ca yamune caiva godāvari sarasvati
narmade sindhu kāveri jale-asmin sannidhiṃ kuru

oṃ the Ganges, Yamuna, Godāvari, Saraswati, Narmada, Sindhu, Kāveri these waters are mingled together.

Note. The Ganges is the Iḍa, Yamuna is the Pingalā. The other five rivers are the five senses. The land of the seven rivers is within the body as well as outside.

Offer 3 flowers into the water pot with the mantra

एते गन्धपुष्पे ॐ गं गणपतये नमः

ete gandhapuṣpe oṃ gaṃ gaṇapataye namaḥ

With these scented flowers oṃ we bow to the Lord of Wisdom, Lord of the Multitudes.

Wave right hand in aṅkuṣa mudrā while chanting this mantra.

ॐ गङ्गे च यमुने चैव गोदावरि सरस्वति ।

नर्मदे सिन्धुकावेरि जलेऽस्मिन् सन्निधि कुरु ॥

oṃ gaṅge ca yamune caiva
godāvari sarasvati
narmade sindhu kāveri jale-asmin sannidhiṃ kuru

oṃ the Ganges, Yamuna, Godāvari, Saraswati, Narmada, Sindhu, Kāveri these waters are mingled together.

ॐ गं गणपतये नमः (Chant 10 times)

oṃ gaṃ gaṇapataye namaḥ

oṃ we bow to the Lord of Wisdom, Lord of the Multitudes.

Sprinkle water over all articles to be offered, then throw some drops of water over your shoulders repeating the mantra:

अमृताम् कुरु स्वाहा

amritām kuru svāhā

Make this immortal nectar! I am One with God!

Puṣpa Śuddhi

Wave hands over flowers with prārthana mudrā while chanting first line and with dhenu mudrā while chanting second line of this mantra.

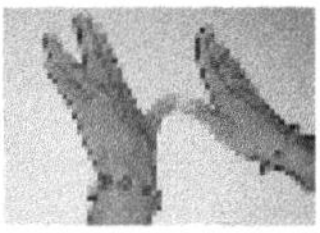

ॐ पुष्प पुष्प महापुष्प सुपुष्प पुष्पसम्भवे ।

पुष्प चयावकीर्णे च हूं फट् स्वाहा ॥

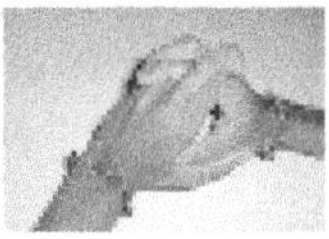

oṃ puṣpa puṣpa mahā puṣpa
supuṣpa puṣpasambhave
puṣpa cayāvakīrṇe ca hūṃ phaṭ svāhā

oṃ Flowers, flowers, Oh Great Flowers, excellent flowers; flowers in heaps and scattered about, cut the ego, purify, I am One with God!

Offer a flower while chanting each of the following mantras ete gandhapuṣpe

एते गन्धपुष्पे ॐ ह्रीं चण्डिकायै नमः

ete gandhapuṣpe oṃ hrīṃ caṇḍikāyai namaḥ

With these scented flowers oṃ I bow to She Who Tears Apart Thought

एते गन्धपुष्पे ॐ ह्रीं श्रीं दुं दुर्गायै नमः

ete gandhapuṣpe oṃ hrīṃ śrīṃ duṃ durgāyai namaḥ

With these scented flowers oṃ I bow to the Reliever of Difficulties

एते गन्धपुष्पे ॐ क्रीं काल्यै नमः

ete gandhapuṣpe oṃ krīṃ kālyai namaḥ

With these scented flowers oṃ I bow to the She Who Is Beyond Time (also the Goddess Who Takes Away Darkness)

एते गन्धपुष्पे ॐ श्रीं लक्ष्म्यै नमः

ete gandhapuṣpe oṃ śrīṃ lakṣmyai namaḥ

With these scented flowers oṃ I bow to the Goddess of True Wealth

एते गन्धपुष्पे ॐ सं सरस्वत्यै नमः

ete gandhapuṣpe oṃ saṃ sarasvatyai namaḥ

With these scented flowers oṃ I bow to the Spirit of All-Pervading Knowledge

एते गन्धपुष्पे ॐ बौं ब्रह्मणे नमः

ete gandhapuṣpe oṃ bauṃ brahmaṇe namaḥ

With these scented flowers oṃ I bow to the Creative Consciousness

एते गन्धपुष्पे ॐ क्लीं विष्णवे नमः

ete gandhapuṣpe oṃ klīṃ viṣṇave namaḥ

With these scented flowers oṃ I bow to the Consciousness Which Pervades All

एते गन्धपुष्पे ॐ नमः शिवाय

ete gandhapuṣpe oṃ namaḥ śivāya

With these scented flowers oṃ I bow to the Consciousness of Infinite Goodness

gaṇeśa gāyatrī

ॐ तत् पुरुषाय विद्महे वक्रतुण्डाय धीमहि ।

तन्नो दन्ती प्रचोदयात् ॥

oṃ tat puruṣāya vidmahe vakratuṇḍāya dhīmahi
tanno dantī pracodayāt

oṃ we meditate upon that Perfect Consciousness, contemplate the One with a broken tooth. May that One with the Great Tusk grant us increase.

एते गन्धपुष्पे ॐ गं गणपतये नमः

ete gandhapuṣpe oṃ gaṃ gaṇapataye namaḥ

With these scented flowers oṃ we bow to the Lord of Wisdom, Lord of the Multitudes.

gaṇeśa dhyānam

meditation

ॐ खर्व्वं स्थूलतनुं गजेन्द्रवदनं लम्बोदरं सुन्दरं

प्रस्यन्दन्मदगन्धलुब्धमधुपव्यालोलगण्डस्थलम् ।

दन्ताघातविदारितारिरुधिरैः सिन्दूरशोभाकरं

वन्दे शैलसुतासुतं गणपतिं सिद्धिप्रदं कामदं ॥

oṃ kharvvaṃ sthūlatanuṃ gajendravadanaṃ
lambodaraṃ sundaraṃ
prasyandanmadagandhalubdhamadhupavyālolagaṇḍasth
alam
dantāghātavidāritārirudhiraiḥ sindūraśobhākaraṃ
vande śailasutāsutaṃ gaṇapatiṃ siddhipradaṃ
kāmadaṃ

Gaṇeśa Pūjā

oṃ Gaṇeśa, the Lord of Wisdom, is short, of stout body, with the face of the king of elephants and a big belly and is extemely beautiful. From whom pours forth an etherial fluid, the sweet fragrance of which has captivated with love the bees who are swarming about his cheeks. With the blows of his tusks he pierces all enemies, and he is beautified by red vermillion. We bow with praise to the son of the daughter of the Mountains, Pārvatī, the daughter of Himalayas, the Lord of the Multitudes, the Giver of Perfection of all desires.

ॐ गं गणेशाय नमः

oṃ gaṃ gaṇeśāya namaḥ

oṃ We bow to Gaṇeśa, the Lord of Wisdom, Lord of the Multitudes.

kara nyāsa

establishment in the hands

ॐ गां अंगुष्ठाभ्यां नमः

oṃ gāṃ aṃguṣṭhābhyāṃ namaḥ thumb forefinger

oṃ Gaṃ in the thumb I bow.

ॐ गीं तर्जनीभ्यां स्वाहा

oṃ gīṃ tarjanībhyāṃ svāhā thumb forefinger

oṃ Gīṃ in the forefinger, I am One with God!

ॐ गूं मद्यमाभ्यां वषट्

oṃ gūṃ madyamābhyāṃ vaṣaṭ thumb middlefinger

oṃ Gūṃ in the middle finger, Purify!

ॐ गैं अनामिकाभ्यां हुं

oṃ gaiṃ anāmikābhyāṃ huṃ thumb ringfinger

oṃ Gaiṃ in the ring finger, Cut the Ego!

ॐ गौं कनिष्ठिकाभ्यां वौषट्

oṃ gauṃ kaniṣṭhikābyāṃ vauṣaṭ thumb littlefinger
oṃ Gauṃ in the little finger, Ultimate Purity!

Roll hand over hand forwards while reciting *karatala kara* and backwards while chanting *pṛṣṭhābhyāṃ*, then clap hands when chanting *astrāya phaṭ*.

ॐ गः करतल कर पृष्ठाभ्यां अस्त्राय फट्

oṃ gaḥ karatala kara pṛṣṭhābhyāṃ astrāya phaṭ
oṃ Gaḥ roll hand over hand front and back and clap with the weapon of Virtue.

ॐ गं गणेशाय नमः

oṃ gaṃ gaṇeśāya namaḥ
oṃ We bow to Gaṇeśa, the Lord of Wisdom, Lord of the Multitudes.

aṅga nyāsa

establishment in the body

Holding tattva mudrā, touch heart.

ॐ गां हृदयाय नमः

oṃ gāṃ hṛdayāya namaḥ touch heart
oṃ Gaṃ in the heart, I bow.

Holding tattva mudrā, touch top of head.

ॐ गीं शिरसे स्वाहा

oṃ gīṃ śirase svāhā top of head
oṃ Gīṃ on the top of the head, I am One with God!

Gaṇeśa Pūjā

With thumb extended, touch back of head.

ॐ गूं शिखायै वषट्

oṃ gūṃ śikhāyai vaṣaṭ back of head

oṃ Gūṃ on the back of the head, Purify!

Holding tattva mudrā, cross both arms.

ॐ गैं कवचाय हुं

oṃ gaiṃ kavacāya huṃ cross both arms

oṃ Gaiṃ crossing both arms, Cut the Ego!

Holding tattva mudrā, touch three eyes at once with three middle fingers.

ॐ गौं नेत्रत्रयाय वौषट्

oṃ gauṃ netratrayāya vauṣaṭ touch three eyes

oṃ Gauṃ in the three eyes, Ultimate Purity!

Roll hand over hand forwards while reciting *karatala kara* and backwards while chanting *pṛṣṭhābhyāṃ*, then clap hands when chanting *astrāya phaṭ*.

ॐ गः करतल कर पृष्ठाभ्यां अस्त्राय फट्

oṃ gaḥ karatala kara pṛṣṭhābhyāṃ astrāya phaṭ

oṃ Gaḥ roll hand over hand front and back and clap with the weapon of Virtue.

ॐ गं गणेशाय नमः

oṃ gaṃ gaṇeśāya namaḥ

oṃ We bow to Gaṇeśa, the Lord of Wisdom, Lord of the Multitudes.

ॐ सुमुखश्चैकदन्तश्च कपिलो गजकर्णकः ।

लम्बोदरश्च विकटो विघ्ननाशो विनायकः ॥

oṃ sumukhaścaika dantaśca kapilo gaja karṇakaḥ
lambodaraśca vikaṭo vighnanāśo vināyakaḥ

He has a beautiful face with only one tooth (or tusk), of red color with elephant ears; with a big belly and a great tooth he destroys all obstacles. He is the Remover of Obstacles.

धूम्रकेतुर्गणाध्यक्षो भालचन्द्रो गजाननः ।

द्वादशैतानि नामानि यः पठेच्छृणुयादपि ॥

dhūmraketurgaṇādhyakṣo bhāla candro gajānanaḥ
dvādaśaitāni nāmāni yaḥ paṭhecchṛṇu yādapi

With a grey banner, the living spirit of the multitudes, having the moon on his forehead, with an elephant's face; whoever will recite or listen to these twelve names

विद्यारम्भे विवाहे च प्रवेशे निर्गमे तथा ।

संग्रामे संकटे चैव विघ्नस्तस्य न जायते ॥

vidyārambhe vivāhe ca praveśe nirgame tathā
saṃgrāme saṃkate caiva vighnastasya na jāyate

at the time of commencing studies, getting married, or upon entering or leaving any place; on a battlefield of war, or in any difficulty, will overcome all obstacles.

शुक्लाम्बरधरं देवं शशिवर्णं चतुर्भुजम् ।

प्रसन्नवदनं ध्यायेत् सर्वविघ्नोपशान्तये ॥

śuklāmbaradharaṃ devaṃ śaśivarṇaṃ caturbhujam
prasannavadanaṃ dhyāyet sarvavighnopaśāntaye

Wearing a white cloth, the God has the color of the moon and four arms. That most pleasing countenance is meditated upon, who gives peace to all difficulties.

अभीप्सितार्थसिद्ध्यर्थं पूजितो यः सुरासुरैः ।
सर्वविघ्नहरस् तस्मै गणाधिपतये नमः ॥

abhīpsitārtha siddhyartham̱ pūjito yaḥ surā suraiḥ
sarvavighna haras tasmai gaṇādhipataye namaḥ

For gaining the desired objective, or for the attainment of perfection, he is worshiped by the Forces of Union and the Forces of Division alike. He takes away all difficulties, and therefore, we bow down in reverance to the Lord of the Multitudes.

ॐ गं गणपतये नमः

oṃ gaṃ gaṇapataye namaḥ

oṃ we bow to the Lord of Wisdom, Lord of the Multitudes.

अथ गणेश्यथर्वशीर्षम् ॥

atha gaṇeśyatharvaśīrṣam

ॐ नमस्ते गणपतये ॥

oṃ namaste gaṇapataye

oṃ I bow to Gaṇapati.

त्वमेव प्रत्यक्षं तत्त्वमसि ॥

tvaṃeva pratyakṣaṃ tattvamasi

You alone are the perceivable form of That Thou art.

त्वमेव केवलं कर्तासि ॥

tvaṃeva kevalaṃ kartāsi
You alone are the Creator.

त्वमेव केवलं धर्तासि ।

tvaṃeva kevalaṃ dhartāsi
You alone are the Supporter.

त्वमेव केवलं हर्तासि ॥

tvaṃeva kevalaṃ hartāsi
You alone are the Dissolver.

त्वमेव सर्वं खल्विदं ब्रह्मासि ॥

tvaṃeva sarvaṃ khalvidaṃ brahmāsi
You alone are the entire unity of God.

- 1 -

त्वं साक्षादात्मासि नित्यं ॥

tvaṃ sākṣhādātmāsi nityaṃ
You are the actual eternal soul.

- 2 -

ऋतं वच्मि ॥ सत्यं वच्मि ॥

ṛtaṃ vacmi satyaṃ vacmi
I speak truth, I speak truth.

अव त्वं मां ॥

ava tvaṃ māṃ
Protect me.

अव वक्तारं ॥

ava vaktāraṃ
Protect my speech.

अव श्रोतारं ॥

ava śrotāraṃ
Protect my hearing.

अव दातारं ॥

ava dātāraṃ
Protect my giving.

अव धातारं ॥

ava dhātāraṃ
Protect my supporting.

अवानूचानम् ॥

ava anūcānam
Protect my learning.

अवशिष्यं ॥

ava śiṣyaṃ
Protect my disciple.

अव पश्चात्तात् ॥

ava paścāttāt
Protect me from behind.

अव पुरस्तात् ॥

ava purastāt
Protect me from the front.

अवोत्तरात्तात् ॥

avottarāttāt
Protect me from the north.

अव दक्षिणात्तात् ॥

ava dakṣiṇāttāt
Protect me from the south.

अव चोर्ध्वात्तात् ॥

ava cordhvāttāt
Protect me from above.

अवाधरात्तात् ॥

ava adharāttāt
Protect me from below.

- 3 -

सर्वतो मां पाहि पाहि समंतात् ॥

sarvato māṃ pāhi pāhi samaṃtāt
Protect me from all around on every side equally.

त्वं वङ्मयस्त्वं चिन्मयः त्वमानन्दमयस्त्वं ब्रह्ममयः ॥

tvaṃ vaṅmayastvaṃ cinmayaḥ tvamānandamayastvaṃ brahmamayaḥ
You are the manifestation of sound, the manifestation of consciousness, the manifestation of bliss, the manifestation of Supreme Divinity.

त्वं सच्चिदानन्दाद्वितीयोऽसि ॥

tvaṃ saccidānandadvitīyo-si

You are Truth, Consciousness and Bliss beyond duality.

त्वं प्रत्यक्षं ब्रह्मासि ॥

tvaṃ pratyakṣaṃ brahmāsi

You are the perceivable Brahma (Supreme Divinity).

- 4 -

त्वं ज्ञानमयो विज्ञानमयोऽसि ॥

tvaṃ jñānamayo vijñānamayo-si

You are the manifestation of wisdom and knowledge.

सर्वं जगदिदं त्वत्तो जायते ॥

sarvaṃ jagadidaṃ tvatto jāyate

All of this perceivable universe is brought forth from you.

सर्वं जगदिदं त्वत्तस्तिष्ठति ॥

sarvaṃ jagadidaṃ tvattastiṣṭhati

All of this perceivable universe has its existence in you.

सर्वं जगदिदं त्वयि लयमेष्यति ॥

sarvaṃ jagadidaṃ tvayi layameṣyati

All of this perceivable universe will dissolve its existence in you.

सर्वं जगदिदं त्वयि प्रत्येति ॥

sarvaṃ jagadidaṃ tvayi pratyeti

All of this perceivable universe will return to you.

त्वं भूमिरापोऽनलोऽनिलो नमः ॥

tvaṃ bhūmirāpo-nalo-nilo namaḥ

I bow to you as the earth, water, fire, wind.

- 5 -

त्वं चत्वारि वाक्पदानि ॥

tvaṃ catvāri vākpadāni

You are the meeting place of the syllables of speech.

त्वं गुणत्रयातीतः ॥

tvaṃ guṇatrayātītaḥ

You are beyond the three qualities.

त्वं देहत्रयातीतः ॥

tvaṃ dehatrayātītaḥ

You are beyond the three bodies (gross, subtle and causal).

त्वं कालत्रयातीतः ॥

tvaṃ kālatrayātītaḥ

You are beyond the three times.

त्वं मूलाधार स्थितोऽसि नित्यम् ॥

tvaṃ mūlādhāra stitho-si nityam

You reside eternally in the mūlādhāra cakra.

त्वं शक्तित्रयात्मकः ॥

tvaṃ śaktitrayātmakaḥ

You are the soul of the three energies.

त्वां योगिनो ध्यायन्ति नित्यम् ॥

tvāṃ yogino dhyāyanti nityam

Yogis continually meditate upon you.

\- 6 -

त्वं ब्रह्मा त्वं विष्णुस्त्वं रुद्रस्त्वमिंद्रस्त्वमग्निस्त्वं वायुस्त्वं सूर्यस्त्वं चन्द्रमास्त्वं ब्रह्म भूर्भुवः स्वरोम् ॥

tvaṃ brahmā tvaṃ viṣṇustvaṃ rudrastvamiṃdrastvam agnistvaṃ vāyustvaṃ sūryastvam candramāstvaṃ brahma bhūr bhuvaḥ svarom

You are Brahmā, Viṣṇu, Rudra, Indra, Agni, Vāyu, Sūrya, Chandramā, the Unknowable Divinity who pervades the three worlds and beyond.

गणादिं पूर्वमुच्चार्य वर्णादिं तदनन्तरम् ॥

gaṇādiṃ pūrvamuccārya varṇādiṃ tadanantaram

These are the instructions for the full correct pronunciation of the letters of the Ganeśa mantras of that Supreme Soul (literally, that which is uninterrupted).

अनुस्वारः परतरः ॥

anusvāraḥ parataraḥ

Anusvāraḥ (ṃ) comes last.

अर्धेदुलसितम् ॥

ardhedulasitam

The half moon (m̐) plays

तारेण रुद्धम् ॥

tāreṇa ruddham

with the Tārā (oṃ), which it checks or restrains.

एतत्तव मनोस्वरूपम् ॥

ettattava manosvarūpam
And this is the intrinsic nature of the manifestations of mind.

गकारःपूर्वरूपम् ॥

gakāraḥ pūrvarūpam
In the beginning is the letter G.

अकारो मध्यमरूपम् ॥

akāro madhyamarūpam
In the middle is the letter a.

अनुस्वारश्चान्त्यरूपम् ॥

anusvāraścāntyarūpam
Anusvāraḥ (ṃ) is the form at the end.

बिन्दुरुत्तररूपम् ॥

binduruttararūpam
Bindu (ṃ) is the form above.

नादः संधानम् ॥

nādaḥ saṃdhānam
The subtle sound is joined together

संहिता संधिः ॥

saṃhitā saṃdhiḥ
according to the rules of the union of letters in literature.

सैषा गणेशविद्या ॥

saiṣā gaṇeśavidyā
This is the knowledge of the mantra of Ganeśa.

गणक ऋषिः ॥

gaṇaka ṛṣiḥ
Ganak is the Ṛṣi.

निचृद्गायत्रीच्छन्दः ॥

nicṛid gāyatrīcchandaḥ
Nicṛd Gāyatrī is the rhythm.

गणपतिर्देवता ॥

gaṇapatirdevatā
Gaṇapati is the devatā.

- 7 -

ॐ गं गणपतये नमः ॥

oṃ gaṃ gaṇapataye namaḥ
oṃ Gaṃ I bow to Gaṇapati.

एकदन्ताय विद्महे वक्रतुण्डाय धीमहि ।
तन्नो दन्तिः प्रचोदयात् ॥

ekadantāya vidmahe vakratuṇḍāya dhīmahi
tanno dantiḥ pracodayāt
We know He with one tooth, meditate upon He with the bent tusk.
May He (of the special tooth) grant us increase.

एकदन्तं चतुर्हस्तं पाशमंकुशधारिणम् ।

रदं च वरचं हस्तैर्ब्रिभ्राणं मूषकध्वजम् ॥

ekadantaṃ caturhastaṃ pāśamaṃkuśadhāriṇam
radaṃ ca varacaṃ hastair bribhrāṇaṃ mūṣakadhvajam

He has one tooth and four hands. He holds a net, a goad, an elephant's tusk and the mudrā which grants boons, bearing a banner upon which is the emblem of a mouse.

रक्तं लंबोदरं शर्पकर्णकं रक्तवाससम् ।

रक्तगन्धानुलिप्तांगं रक्तपुष्पैः सुपूजितम् ॥

raktaṃ laṃbodaraṃ śarpakarṇakam raktavāsasam
raktagandhānuliptāṃgaṃ raktapuṣpaiḥ supūjitam

His body is red, his belly big, his ears are like great fans and his clothing red. His body is covered with red unguents, and He is worshiped with red flowers.

भक्तानुकंपिनं देवं जगत्कारणमच्युतम् ।

आविर्भूतं च सृष्ट्यादौ प्रकृतेः पुरुषात्परम् ॥

bhaktānukaṃpinaṃ devaṃ jagatkāraṇamacyutam
āvirbhūtaṃ ca sṛistyādau prakṛteḥ puruṣātparam

He is the God who is gracious to devotees and the primary cause of perceivable existence. His presence was manifest before creation. He is beyond both Puruṣa and Prakṛti.

एवं ध्यायति यो नित्यं स योगी योगिनां वरः ॥ ८

evaṃ dhyāyati yo nityaṃ sa yogī yogināṃ varaḥ

And whoever continually meditates in this way is blessed. He becomes the Yogi of all Yogis.

नमो व्रातपतये नमो गणपतये नमः प्रमथपतये नमस्तेऽस्तु

लंबोदराय एकदन्ताय विघ्ननाशिने शिवसुताय श्रीवरदमूर्तये

नमः ॥ ९

namo vrātapataye namo gaṇapataye namaḥ pramathapataye namaste-stu lambodarāya ekadantāya vighnanāśine śivasutāya śrīvaradamūrtaye namaḥ

I bow to the Lord of all Vows, to the Lord of the Multitudes, to the Lord who is foremost. I bow to the Lord with a big belly, with one tooth, who removes all obstacles, to the son of Śiva, to the Divine One who grants boons.

इदमथर्वशीर्षं योऽधीते स ब्रह्मभूयाय कल्पते ॥

idamatharvaśīrṣaṃ yo-dhīte sa brahmabhūyāya kalpate

Who studies the "Highest Meaning" conceives himself to be one with God.

स सर्वविघ्नैर्न बाध्यते ॥

sa sarvavighnairna bādhyate

No obstacle can bind him.

स सर्गतः सुखमेधते ॥

sa sargataḥ sukhamedhate

His loving intellect reflects the happiness of heaven.

स पञ्चमहापापात्प्रमुच्यते ॥

sa pañcamahāpāpātpramucyate

He removes the five great kinds of sin.

सायमधीयानो दिवसकृतं पापं नाशयति ॥

sāyamadhīyāno divasakṛtaṃ pāpaṃ nāśayati

Who contemplates (this knowledge) in the night, is freed from sins committed in the day.

प्रातरधीयानो रात्रिकृतं पापं नाशयति ॥

prātaradhīyāno rātrikṛtaṃ pāpaṃ nāśayati

Who contemplates (this knowledge) in the day, is freed from sins committed in the night.

सायंप्रातः प्रयुंजानो अपापो भवति ॥

sāyaṃprātaḥ prayuṃjāno apāpo bhavati

Who contemplates (this knowledge) in the night and in the day, is freed from all sins.

सर्वत्रा धीयानोऽपविघ्नो भवति ॥

sarvatrā dhīyāno-pavighno bhavati

Who always contemplates (this knowledge), is freed from all obstacles,

धर्मार्थकाममोक्षं च विदति ॥

dharmārthakāmamokṣaṃ ca vidati

and he knows dharma (the way of truth and harmony, artha (the necessities of life), Kāma (the purification of all desires), and Mokṣa (liberation, otherwise known as self-realization).

इदमथर्वशीर्षमशिष्याय न देयम् ॥

idamatharvaśīrṣamaśiṣyāya na deyam

This "Highest Meaning" should not be given to one who is not a disciple,

यो यदि मोहाद्दात्यति स पापीयान् भवति ॥

yo yadi mohāddātyati sa pāpīyān bhavati

nor to one who is ignorant. Such giving is a sin

सहस्रावर्तनात् ॥

sahasrāvartanāt

from which extreme bad fortune arises.

यं यं काममधीते तं तमनेन साधयेत् ॥

yaṃ yaṃ kāmamadhīte taṃ tamanena sādhayet

Wherever desires are contemplated, immediately they will be fulfilled.

अनेन गणपतिमभिषिंचति स वाग्भीभवति ॥

anena gaṇapatimabhiṣiṃcati sa vāgbhībhavati

Gaṇapati will make him without fault. He will become one with knowledge and vibrations.

चतुर्थ्यामनुस्थानम् जपति स विद्यावान्भवति ॥

caturthyāmanusthānam japati sa vidyāvānbhavati

If he will recite at the fourth time of prayer, he will become full of knowledge.

इत्यथर्वण वाक्यम् ॥

ityatharvaṇa vākyam

This is the word of Atharvaṇ (a name of Śiva).

ब्रह्माद्याचरणं विद्यात् न विभेति कदाचनेति ॥

brahmādyācaraṇaṃ vidyāt na vibheti kadācaneti

He will know only divine behavior, etc., and will never act contrarily.

यो दूर्वांकुरैर्यजति स वैश्रवणोपमो भवति

यो लाजैर्यजति स यशोबान्भवति स मेधावान्भवति ॥

yo dūrvāṃkurairyajati sa vaiśravaṇopamo bhavati
yo lājairyajati sa yaśobānbhavati sa medhāvānbhavati

Whoever offers sprouts of durva grass becomes elevated in the universe. Whoever offers flattened rice becomes a repository of fame and welfare, becomes filled with loving intellect.

यो मोदकसहस्रेण यजति स वाञ्छितफलमवाप्नोति ।

यः सत्यसमिद्भिर्यजति स सर्वं लभते स सर्वं लभते ॥

yo modakasahasreṇa yajati
sa vāñchitaphalamavāpnoti
yaḥ satyasamidbhiryajati sa sarvaṃ labhate
sa sarvaṃ labhate

Whoever offers a thousand sweets, attains his desired objective. Whoever offers the worship with truth attains all, attains all.

अष्टो ब्राह्मणान् सम्यग्राहायत्वा सूर्यवर्चस्वी भवति ।

सूर्यग्रहे महानद्यां प्रतिमासन्निधौ वा जप्वा सिद्धमन्त्रो

भवति ॥

aṣṭo brāhmaṇān samyagrāhāyatvā sūryavarcasvī bhavati
sūryagrahe mahānadyāṃ pratimāsannidhau vā japvā
siddhamantro bhavati

Whoever offers to eight Brahmaṇs for their acceptance, becomes an offeror of the Light of Wisdom. At the time of solar eclipse, on the banks of great rivers, if one recites, he becomes perfect in mantras.

महाविघ्नात्प्रमुच्यते ॥

mahāvighnātpramucyate
Great obstacles are removed.

महादोषात्प्रमुच्यते ॥

mahādoṣātpramucyate
Great faults are removed.

स सर्वविद्भवति स सर्वविद्भवति ।

य एवं वेद । इत्युपनिषद् ॥

sa sarvavidbhavati sa sarvavidbhavati
ya evaṃ veda ityupaniṣad
He becomes a knower of all. He becomes a knower of all. And this is the wisdom. Thus ends the Upaniṣad.

ॐ सह नाववतु ॥ सह नौ भुनक्तु ॥

सहवीर्यं करवावहै ॥ तेजस्वि नावधीतमस्तु ॥

मा विद्विषावहै ॥

ॐ शान्तिः । ॐ शान्तिः । ॐ शान्तिः ॥

oṃ saha nāvavatu saha nau bhunaktu
sahavīryaṃ karavāvahai tejasvi nāvadhītamastu mā vidviṣāvahai
oṃ śāntiḥ oṃ śāntiḥ oṃ śāntiḥ
oṃ May the Lord protect us. May the Lord grant us enjoyment of all actions. May we be granted strength to work together. May our studies be thorough and faithful. May all disagreement cease.

गणेश शतनाम

one hundred eight names of gaṇeśa

\- 1 -

ॐ विनायकाय नमः

oṃ vināyakāya namaḥ

Oṃ We bow to he who is the Remover of Obstacles

\- 2 -

ॐ विघ्नराजाय नमः

oṃ vighnarājāya namaḥ

Oṃ We bow to he who is the King of Difficulties

\- 3 -

ॐ गौरीपुत्राय नमः

oṃ gaurīputrāya namaḥ

Oṃ We bow to he who is the son of She who is Rays of Light

\- 4 -

ॐ गणेश्वराय नमः

oṃ gaṇeśvarāya namaḥ

Oṃ We bow to he who is the Lord of Wisdom, Lord of the Multitudes

\- 5 -

ॐ स्कन्दाग्रजाय नमः

oṃ skandāgrajāya namaḥ

Oṃ We bow to he who came before Kartikeya

\- 6 -

ॐ अव्ययाय नमः

oṃ avyayāya namaḥ

Oṃ We bow to he who is the Unchangeable One

\- 7 -

ॐ पूत्राय नमः

oṃ pūtrāya namaḥ

Oṃ We bow to he who is the Son

\- 8 -

ॐ दक्षाय नमः

oṃ dakṣāya namaḥ

Oṃ We bow to he who has Ability

\- 9 -

ॐ अद्यक्षाय नमः

oṃ adhyakṣāya namaḥ

Oṃ We bow to he who Resides in the Now

\- 10 -

ॐ द्विजप्रियाय नमः

oṃ dvijapriyāya namaḥ

Oṃ We bow to he who is the Beloved of the Twice-born

\- 11 -

ॐ अग्निगर्भच्चिदे नमः

oṃ agnigarbhaccide namaḥ

Oṃ We bow to he who pierces the womb of Fire

\- 12 -

ॐ इन्द्रश्रीप्रदाय नमः

oṃ indraśrīpradāya namaḥ

Oṃ We bow to he upon whom Indra bestows the highest respect

\- 13 -

ॐ वाणीप्रदाय नमः

oṃ vāṇīpradāya namaḥ

Oṃ We bow to he who gives all sound

\- 14 -

ॐ अव्ययाय नमः

oṃ avyayāya namaḥ

Oṃ We bow to he who is the Unchangeable One

\- 15 -

ॐ सर्वसिद्धिप्रदाय नमः

oṃ sarvasiddhipradāya namaḥ

Oṃ We bow to he who bestows all attainments of Perfection

\- 16 -

ॐ सर्वतनयाय नमः

oṃ sarvatanayāya namaḥ

Oṃ We bow to he whose entire body is completely reborn

\- 17 -

ॐ शर्वरीप्रियाय नमः

oṃ śarvarīpriyāya namaḥ

Oṃ We bow to he who is beloved by the Star-lit Night

\- 18 -

ॐ सर्वात्मकाय नमः

oṃ sarvatmakāya namaḥ

Oṃ We bow to he who is the Intrinsic Soul of All

\- 19 -

ॐ स्रिष्टिकर्त्रे नमः

oṃ sriṣṭikartre namaḥ

Oṃ We bow to he who conducts Creation

\- 20 -

ॐ देवाय नमः

oṃ devāya namaḥ

Oṃ We bow to he who is the Shining One, the God

- 21 -

ॐ अनेकार्चिताय नमः

oṃ anekārcitāya namaḥ

Oṃ We bow to he who gives many offerings

- 22 -

ॐ शिवाय नमः

oṃ śivāya namaḥ

Oṃ We bow to he who is the Consciousness of Infinite Goodness

- 23 -

ॐ शुद्धाय नमः

oṃ śuddhāya namaḥ

Oṃ We bow to he who is Pure

- 24 -

ॐ बुद्धिप्रियाय नमः

oṃ buddhipriyāya namaḥ

Oṃ We bow to he who is the Beloved of Intelligence

- 25 -

ॐ शान्ताय नमः

oṃ śāntāya namaḥ

Oṃ We bow to he who is Peace

- 26 -

ॐ ब्रह्मचारिणे नमः

oṃ brahmacāriṇe namaḥ

Oṃ We bow to he who Moves in Consciousness

- 27 -

ॐ गजाननाय नमः

oṃ gajānanāya namaḥ

Oṃ We bow to he who has the face of an Elephant

- 28 -

ॐ द्वैमात्रेयाय नमः

oṃ dvaimātreyāya namaḥ

Oṃ We bow to he who has two Mothers

- 29 -

ॐ मुनिस्तुत्याय नमः

oṃ munistutyāya namaḥ

Oṃ We bow to he whose praise is sung by munis

- 30 -

ॐ भक्तविघ्नविनाशनाय नमः

oṃ bhaktavighnavināśanāya namaḥ

Oṃ We bow to he who Destroys all obstacles for Devotees

- 31 -

ॐ एकदन्ताय नमः

oṃ ekadantāya namaḥ

Oṃ We bow to he who has one tooth

- 32 -

ॐ चतुर्बाहवे नमः

oṃ caturbāhave namaḥ

Oṃ We bow to he who has four arms

- 33 -

ॐ चतुराय नमः

oṃ caturāya namaḥ

Oṃ We bow to he who is the Four

- 34 -

ॐ शक्तिसम्युक्ताय नमः

oṃ śaktisamyuktāya namaḥ

Oṃ We bow to he who is United with Energy

- 35 -

ॐ लम्बोदराय नमः

oṃ lambodarāya namaḥ

Oṃ We bow to he who has a big belly

- 36 -

ॐ शूर्पकुराय नमः

oṃ śūrpakurāya namaḥ

Oṃ We bow to he whose ears are like a winnowing fan

- 37 -

ॐ हरये नमः

oṃ haraye namaḥ

Oṃ We bow to he who takes away

- 38 -

ॐ ब्रह्मविदुत्तमाय नमः

oṃ brahmaviduttamāya namaḥ

Oṃ We bow to he who is the Ambassador of Consciousness

- 39 -

ॐ कालाय नमः

oṃ kālāya namaḥ

Oṃ We bow to he who is Time

- 40 -

ॐ ग्रहपतये नमः

oṃ grahapataye namaḥ

Oṃ We bow to he who is the Lord of the Cosmos

- 41 -

ॐ कामिने नमः

oṃ kāmine namaḥ

Oṃ We bow to he who is the Embodiment of Desire

- 42 -

ॐ सोमसूर्याग्निलोचनाय नमः

oṃ somasūryāgnilocanāya namaḥ

Oṃ We bow to he whose three eyes are the Moon, the Sun and Fire

- 43 -

ॐ पाशाण्कुशधराय नमः

oṃ pāśāṇkuśadharāya namaḥ

Oṃ We bow to he who holds the net and curved sword

- 44 -

ॐ चण्डाय नमः

oṃ caṇḍāya namaḥ

Oṃ We bow to he who gets angry

- 45 -

ॐ गुणातीताय नमः

oṃ guṇātītāya namaḥ

Oṃ We bow to he who is Beyond Quality

- 46 -

ॐ निरञ्जनाय नमः

oṃ nirañjanāya namaḥ

Oṃ We bow to he who is Spotless and Pure

- 47 -

ॐ अकल्मषाय नमः

oṃ akalmaṣāya namaḥ

Oṃ We bow to he who is Spotless without stain

- 48 -

ॐ स्वयंसिद्धाय नमः

oṃ svayaṃsiddhāya namaḥ

Oṃ We bow to he who himself is perfect

- 49 -

ॐ सिद्धार्चितपदाम्बुजाय नमः

oṃ siddhārcitapadāmbujāya namaḥ

Oṃ We bow to he whose arms and legs are worshipped by Siddhas

- 50 -

ॐ बीजपूरफलाशक्ताय नमः

oṃ bījapūraphalāśaktāya namaḥ

Oṃ We bow to he whose energy transforms a seed into a fully ripened fruit

- 51 -

ॐ वरदाय नमः

oṃ varadāya namaḥ

Oṃ We bow to he who gives boons

- 52 -

ॐ षाश्वताय नमः

oṃ ṣāśvatāya namaḥ

Oṃ We bow to he who gives boons

- 53 -

ॐ कृतिने नमः

oṃ kṛtine namaḥ

Oṃ We bow to he who performs Karma

- 54 -

ॐ द्विजप्रियाय नमः

oṃ dvijapriyāya namaḥ

Oṃ We bow to he who is the beloved of the Twice Born

- 55 -

ॐ वीतभयाय नमः

oṃ vītabhayāya namaḥ

Oṃ We bow to he who is Free from fear

\- 56 -

ॐ गदिने नमः

oṃ gadine namaḥ

Oṃ We bow to he who holds the club

\- 57 -

ॐ चक्रिणे नमः

oṃ cakriṇe namaḥ

Oṃ We bow to he who holds the discus

\- 58 -

ॐ इक्षुचापधृते नमः

oṃ ikṣucāpadhṛte namaḥ

Oṃ We bow to he who bends the bow of sugar cane

\- 59 -

ॐ श्रीदाय नमः

oṃ śrīdāya namaḥ

Oṃ We bow to he who gives the Highest Respect

\- 60 -

ॐ अजाय नमः

oṃ ajāya namaḥ

Oṃ We bow to he who is Unborn

\- 61 -

ॐ उत्पलकराय नमः

oṃ utpalakarāya namaḥ

Oṃ We bow to he who is the Maker of Flowers

\- 62 -

ॐ श्रीपतये नमः

oṃ śrīpataye namaḥ

Oṃ We bow to he who is the Lord of the Highest Respect

- 63 -

ॐ स्तुतिहर्षिताय नमः

oṃ stutiharṣitāya namaḥ

Oṃ We bow to he who is the Recipient of all Songs

- 64 -

ॐ कुलादिभेत्रे नमः

oṃ kulādibhetre namaḥ

Oṃ We bow to he who distinguishes different communities

- 65 -

ॐ जटिलाय नमः

oṃ jaṭilāya namaḥ

Oṃ We bow to he whose hair is matted

- 66 -

ॐ कलिकल्मषनाशनाय नमः

oṃ kalikalmaṣanāśanāya namaḥ

Oṃ We bow to he who is the Destroyer of the Darkness of Kali (the Dark Age)

- 67 -

ॐ चन्द्रचूडामणये नमः

oṃ candracūḍāmaṇaye namaḥ

Oṃ We bow to he who wears the Moon as a gem in his crown

- 68 -

ॐ कान्ताय नमः

oṃ kāntāya namaḥ

Oṃ We bow to he who is Beautiful

- 69 -

ॐ पापहारिणे नमः

oṃ pāpahāriṇe namaḥ

Oṃ We bow to he who Takes away Sin

- 70 -

ॐ समाहिताय नमः

oṃ samāhitāya namaḥ

Oṃ We bow to he who unites All

- 71 -

ॐ आश्रिताय नमः

oṃ āśritāya namaḥ

Oṃ We bow to he upon whom all are dependent

- 72 -

ॐ श्रीकराय नमः

oṃ śrīkarāya namaḥ

Oṃ We bow to he who Causes the Ultimate Prosperity

- 73 -

ॐ सौम्याय नमः

oṃ saumyāya namaḥ

Oṃ We bow to he who is Beautiful

- 74 -

ॐ भक्तवान्चितदायकाय नमः

oṃ bhaktavāncitadāyakāya namaḥ

Oṃ We bow to he who gives certainty to devotees

- 75 -

ॐ शान्ताय नमः

oṃ śāntāya namaḥ

Oṃ We bow to he who is peace

- 76 -

ॐ कैवल्यसुखदाय नमः

oṃ kaivalyasukhadāya namaḥ

Oṃ We bow to he who gives Unlimited Comfort

\- 77 -

ॐ सच्चिदानन्दविग्रहाय नमः

oṃ saccidānandavigrahāya namaḥ

Oṃ We bow to he who divides the Infinite Existence-Consciousness-Bliss

\- 78 -

ॐ ज्ञानिने नमः

oṃ jñānine namaḥ

Oṃ We bow to he who is the Wise One

\- 79 -

ॐ दयायुताय नमः

oṃ dayāyutāya namaḥ

Oṃ We bow to he who gives Compassion

\- 80 -

ॐ दान्ताय नमः

oṃ dāntāya namaḥ

Oṃ We bow to he who has great teeth

\- 81 -

ॐ ब्रह्मद्वेषविवर्जिताय नमः

oṃ brahmadveṣavivarjitāya namaḥ

Oṃ We bow to he who prohibits the hatred of Supreme Divinity

\- 82 -

ॐ प्रमत्तदैत्यभयदाय नमः

oṃ pramattadaityabhayadāya namaḥ

Oṃ We bow to he who gives excessive fear to the forces of duality

\- 83 -

ॐ श्रीकण्ठाय नमः

oṃ śrīkaṇṭhāya namaḥ

Oṃ We bow to he who has a beautiful throat

\- 84 -

ॐ विभुदेश्वराय नमः

oṃ vibhudeśvarāya namaḥ

Oṃ We bow to he who is the All-Pervading Lord

\- 85 -

ॐ रमार्चिताय नमः

oṃ ramārcitāya namaḥ

Oṃ We bow to he who offers with Delight

\- 86 -

ॐ विधये नमः

oṃ vidhaye namaḥ

Oṃ We bow to he who is worshiped

\- 87 -

ॐ नागराजयज्ञोपवीतवते नमः

oṃ nāgarājayajñopavītavate namaḥ

Oṃ We bow to he who gives the sacred thread to the King of the City

\- 88 -

ॐ स्थूलकण्ठाय नमः

oṃ sthūlakaṇṭhāya namaḥ

Oṃ We bow to he who has a great throat

\- 89 -

ॐ स्वयम्कर्त्रे नमः

oṃ svayamkartre namaḥ

Oṃ We bow to he who does Himself

\- 90 -

ॐ सामघोषप्रियाय नमः

oṃ sāmaghoṣapriyāya namaḥ

Oṃ We bow to he who loves Songs

\- 91 -

ॐ परस्मै नमः

oṃ parasmai namaḥ

Oṃ We bow to he who is Beyond

\- 92 -

ॐ स्थूलतुण्डाय नमः

oṃ sthūlatuṇḍāya namaḥ

Oṃ We bow to he who has a great snout

\- 93 -

ॐ अग्रण्ये नमः

oṃ agraṇye namaḥ

Oṃ We bow to he who is the Foremost

\- 94 -

ॐ धीराय नमः

oṃ dhīrāya namaḥ

Oṃ We bow to he who is constant

\- 95 -

ॐ वागीशाय नमः

oṃ vāgīśāya namaḥ

Oṃ We bow to he who is the Perceier of all Vibrations

\- 96 -

ॐ सिद्धिदायकाय नमः

oṃ siddhidāyakāya namaḥ

Oṃ We bow to he who is the Giver of all Attainments

\- 97 -

ॐ दूर्वाबिल्वप्रियाय नमः

oṃ dūrvābilvapriyāya namaḥ

Oṃ We bow to he who loves Dūrva grass and Bilva leaves

- 98 -

ॐ अव्यक्तमूर्तये नमः

oṃ avyaktamūrtaye namaḥ

Oṃ We bow to he who is Indistinguishable (Infinite) Image

- 99 -

ॐ अद्भुतमूर्तिमते नमः

oṃ adbhutamūrtimate namaḥ

Oṃ We bow to he who is the Incredible Image

- 100 -

ॐ सैलेन्द्रतनुजोत्संगखेलनोत् सुकमानसाय नमः

oṃ sailendratanujotsaṃgakhelanot sukamānasāya namaḥ

Oṃ We bow to he whose excellent thoughts are playing with the Mountain King (Lord Śiva)

- 101 -

ॐ स्वलावण्यसुधासारजितमन्म उविग्रहाय नमः

oṃ svalāvaṇyasudhāsārajitamanma uvigrahāya namaḥ

Oṃ We bow to he whose own charm extends the distribution of pure desire

- 102 -

ॐ समस्तजगदाधाराय नमः

oṃ samastajagadādhārāya namaḥ

Oṃ We bow to he who supports all the Worlds

- 103 -

ॐ मायिने नमः

oṃ māyine namaḥ

Oṃ We bow to he who Measures

\- 104 -

ॐ मूषिकवाहनाय नमः

oṃ mūṣikavāhanāya namaḥ

Oṃ We bow to he who rides on a mouse

\- 105 -

ॐ हृष्टाय नमः

oṃ hṛṣṭāya namaḥ

Oṃ We bow to he who is thrilled with Joy

\- 106 -

ॐ तुष्टाय नमः

oṃ tuṣṭāya namaḥ

Oṃ We bow to he who is Satisfied

\- 107 -

ॐ प्रसन्नात्मने नमः

oṃ prasannātmane namaḥ

Oṃ We bow to he whose soul is delighted

\- 108 -

ॐ सर्वसिद्धिप्रदायकाय

oṃ sarvasiddhipradāyakāya namaḥ

Oṃ We bow to he who is the Bestower of all attainments of perfection

ॐ नमः इति

oṃ namaḥ iti

And that is the end.

वक्रतुण्ड महाकाय सूर्यकोटिसमप्रभ ।

अविघ्नं कुरु मे देव सर्वकार्येषु सर्वदा ॥

vakratuṇḍa mahākāya sūrya koṭi samaprabha
avighnaṃ kuru me deva sarva kāryeṣu sarvadā

With a broken (or bent) tusk, a great body shining like a million suns, make us free from all obstacles, Oh God. Always remain (with us) in all actions.

एकदन्तं महाकायं लम्बोदरं गजाननम् ।

विघ्ननाशकरं देवं हेरम्बं पणामाम्यहम् ॥

ekadantaṃ mahākāyaṃ lambodaraṃ gajānanam
vighnanāśakaraṃ devaṃ herambaṃ praṇāmāmyaham

With one tooth, a great body, a big belly and an elephant's face, he is the God who destroys all obstacles to whom we are bowing down with devotion.

मल्लिकादि सुगन्धीनि मालित्यादीनि वै प्रभो ।

मयाऽहृतानि पूजार्थं पुष्पाणि प्रतिगृह्यताम् ॥

mallikādi sugandhīni mālityādīni vai prabho
mayā-hṛtāni pūjārthaṃ puṣpāṇi pratigṛhyatām

Various flowers such as mallikā and others of excellent scent, are being offered to you, Our Lord. All these flowers have come from the devotion of our hearts for your worship. Be pleased to accept them.

एते गन्धपुष्पे ॐ गं गणपतये नमः

ete gandhapuṣpe oṃ gaṃ gaṇapataye namaḥ

With these scented flowers oṃ we bow to the Lord of Wisdom, Lord of the Multitudes.

ॐ गं गणपतये नमः

oṃ gaṃ gaṇapataye namaḥ (108 times)
Oṃ we bow to the Lord of Wisdom, Lord of the Multitudes.

If desired, collect the next eight liquid offerings in a bowl.
foot bath

ॐ गं गणपतये नमः पाद्यं समर्पयामि ॥

oṃ gaṃ gaṇapataye namaḥ pādyaṃ samarpayāmi
Oṃ we bow to the Lord of Wisdom, Lord of the Multitudes, and offer these foot bath waters.

milk bath

ॐ गं गणपतये नमः पयः स्नानं समर्पयामि ॥

oṃ gaṃ gaṇapataye namaḥ payaḥ snānaṃ samarpayāmi
Oṃ we bow to the Lord of Wisdom, Lord of the Multitudes, and offer this milk for your bath.

yogurt bath

ॐ गं गणपतये नमः दधि स्नानं समर्पयामि ॥

oṃ gaṃ gaṇapataye namaḥ dadhi snānaṃ samarpayāmi
Oṃ we bow to the Lord of Wisdom, Lord of the Multitudes, and offer this curd for your bath.

ghee bath

ॐ गं गणपतये नमः घृत स्नानं समर्पयामि ॥

oṃ gaṃ gaṇapataye namaḥ ghṛta snānaṃ samarpayāmi
Oṃ we bow to the Lord of Wisdom, Lord of the Multitudes, and offer this ghee for your bath.

honey bath

ॐ गं गणपतये नमः मधु स्नानं समर्पयामि ॥

oṃ gaṃ gaṇapataye namaḥ madhu snānaṃ samarpayāmi

Oṃ we bow to the Lord of Wisdom, Lord of the Multitudes, and offer this honey for your bath.

sugar bath

ॐ गं गणपतये नमः शर्करा स्नानं समर्पयामि ॥

oṃ gaṃ gaṇapataye namaḥ śarkarā snānaṃ samarpayāmi

Oṃ we bow to the Lord of Wisdom, Lord of the Multitudes, and offer this sugar for your bath.

five nectars bath

ॐ गं गणपतये नमः पञ्चामृतं स्नानं समर्पयामि ॥

oṃ gaṃ gaṇapataye namaḥ pañcāmṛtaṃ snānaṃ samarpayāmi

Oṃ we bow to the Lord of Wisdom, Lord of the Multitudes, and offer these five nectars for your bath.

water bath

ॐ गं गणपतये नमः गङ्गा स्नानं समर्पयामि ॥

oṃ gaṃ gaṇapataye namaḥ gaṅgā snānaṃ samarpayāmi

Oṃ we bow to the Lord of Wisdom, Lord of the Multitudes, and offer these bath waters.

cloth

ॐ गं गणपतये नमः वस्त्रां समर्पयामि ॥

oṃ gaṃ gaṇapataye namaḥ vastrāṃ samarpayāmi

Oṃ we bow to the Lord of Wisdom, Lord of the Multitudes, and offer this wearing apparel.

rudrākṣa

ॐ गं गणपतये नमः रुद्राक्षं समर्पयामि ॥

oṃ gaṃ gaṇapataye namaḥ rudrākṣaṃ samarpayāmi

Oṃ we bow to the Lord of Wisdom, Lord of the Multitudes, and offer this rudrākṣa.

red powder

ॐ गं गणपतये नमः सिन्दूरं समर्पयामि ॥

oṃ gaṃ gaṇapataye namaḥ sindūraṃ samarpayāmi

Oṃ we bow to the Lord of Wisdom, Lord of the Multitudes, and offer this red colored powder.

sandal paste

ॐ गं गणपतये नमः चन्दनं समर्पयामि ॥

oṃ gaṃ gaṇapataye namaḥ candanaṃ samarpayāmi

Oṃ we bow to the Lord of Wisdom, Lord of the Multitudes, and offer this sandal paste.

rice

ॐ गं गणपतये नमः अक्षतं समर्पयामि ॥

oṃ gaṃ gaṇapataye namaḥ akṣataṃ samarpayāmi

Oṃ we bow to the Lord of Wisdom, Lord of the Multitudes, and offer these grains of rice.

flower garland

ॐ गं गणपतये नमः पुष्पमाल्लां समर्पयामि ॥

oṃ gaṃ gaṇapataye namaḥ puṣpamālāṃ samārpāyāmi

Oṃ we bow to the Lord of Wisdom, Lord of the Multitudes, and offer this garland of flowers.

food offering

ॐ गं गणपतये नमः भोग नैवेद्यम् समर्पयामि ॥

oṃ gaṃ gaṇapataye namaḥ bhog naivedyam samarpayāmi

Oṃ we bow to the Lord of Wisdom, Lord of the Multitudes, and offer this presentation of food.

drinking water

ॐ गं गणपतये नमः पानार्थ जलम् समर्पयामि ॥

oṃ gaṃ gaṇapataye namaḥ pānārtha jalam samarpayāmi

Oṃ we bow to the Lord of Wisdom, Lord of the Multitudes, and offer this drinking water.

एते गन्धपुष्पे ॐ गं गणपतये नमः

ete gandha puṣpe oṃ gaṃ gaṇapataye namaḥ

With these scented flowers oṃ We bow to the Lord of Wisdom, Lord of the Multitudes.

ॐ गं गणपतये नमः

oṃ gaṃ gaṇapataye namaḥ (108 times)

We bow to the Lord of Wisdom, Lord of the Multitudes.

वक्रतुण्ड महाकाय सूर्यकोटिसमप्रभ ।

अविघ्नं कुरु मे देव सर्वकार्येषु सर्वदा ॥

vakratuṇḍa mahākāya sūrya koṭi samaprabha
avighnaṃ kuru me deva sarva kāryeṣu sarvadā

With a broken (or bent) tusk, a great body shining like a million suns, make us free from all obstacles, Oh God. Always remain (with us) in all actions.

एकदन्तं महाकायं लम्बोदरं गजाननम् ।

विघ्ननाशकरं देवं हेरम्बं प्रणामाम्यहम् ॥

ekadantaṃ mahākāyaṃ lambodaraṃ gajānanam
vighnanāśakaraṃ devaṃ herambaṃ praṇāmāmyaham

With one tooth, a great body, a big belly and an elephant's face, he is the God who destroys all obstacles to whom we are bowing down with devotion.

मल्लिकादि सुगन्धीनि मालित्यादीनि वै प्रभो ।

मयाऽहृतानि पूजार्थं पुष्पाणि प्रतिगृह्यताम् ॥

mallikādi sugandhīni mālityādīni vai prabho
mayā-hṛtāni pūjārthaṃ puṣpāṇi pratigṛhyatām

Various flowers such as mallikā and others of excellent scent, are being offered to you, Our Lord. All these flowers have come from the devotion of our hearts for your worship. Be pleased to accept them.

एते गन्धपुष्पे ॐ गं गणपतये नमः

ete gandhapuṣpe oṃ gaṃ gaṇapataye namaḥ

With these scented flowers oṃ we bow to the Lord of Wisdom, Lord of the Multitudes.

Closing Prayers

दुर्गां शिवां शान्तिकरीं ब्रह्माणीं ब्रह्मणः प्रियाम् ।

सर्वलोक प्रणेत्रीञ्च प्रणमामि सदा शिवाम् ॥

durgāṃ śivāṃ śāntikarīṃ
brahmāṇīṃ brahmaṇaḥ priyām
sarvaloka praṇetrīñca praṇamāmi sadā śivām

The Reliever of Difficulties, Exposer of Goodness, Cause of Peace, Infinite Consciousness, Beloved by Knowers of Consciousness; all the inhabitants of all the worlds always bow to Her, and I am bowing to Goodness Herself.

मङ्गलां शोभनां शुद्धां निष्कलां परमां कलाम् ।

विश्वेश्वरीं विश्वमातां चण्डिकां प्रणमाम्यहम् ॥

maṅgalāṃ śobhanāṃ śuddhāṃ
niṣkalāṃ paramāṃ kalām
viśveśvarīṃ viśvamātāṃ caṇḍikāṃ praṇamāmyaham

Welfare, Radiant Beauty, Completely Pure, Without Limitations, the Ultimate Limitation, the Lord of the Universe, the Mother of the Universe, to you Caṇḍi, to the Energy which Tears Apart Thought, I bow in submission.

सर्वदेवमयीं देवीं सर्वरोगभयापहाम् ।

ब्रह्मेशविष्णुनमितां प्रणमामि सदा शिवाम् ॥

sarvadevamayīṃ devīṃ sarvarogabhayāpahām
brahmeśaviṣṇunamitāṃ praṇamāmi sadā śivām

Composed of all the Gods, removing all sickness and fear, Brahma, Maheshwar and Viṣṇu bow down to Her, and I always bow down to the Energy of Infinite Goodness.

विन्ध्यस्थां विन्ध्यनिलयां दिव्यस्थाननिवासिनीम् ।
योगिनीं योगजननीं चण्डिकां प्रणमाम्यहम् ॥

vindhyasthāṃ vindhyanilayāṃ divyasthānanivāsinīm
yoginīṃ yogajananīṃ caṇḍikāṃ praṇamāmyaham

The dwelling place of Knowledge, residing in Knowledge, Resident in the place of Divine Illumination, the Cause of Union, the Knower of Union, to the Energy Which Tears Apart Thought we constantly bow.

ईशानमातरं देवीमीश्वरीमीश्वरप्रियाम् ।
प्रणतोऽस्मि सदा दुर्गां संसारार्णवतारिणीम् ॥

īśānamātaraṃ devīmīśvarīmīśvarapriyām
praṇato-smi sadā durgāṃ saṃsārārṇavatāriṇīm

The Mother of the Supreme Consciousness, the Goddess Who is the Supreme Consciousness, beloved by the Supreme Consciousness, we always bow to Durgā, the Reliever of Difficulties, who takes aspirants across the difficult sea of objects and their relationships.

ॐ महादेव महात्रान महायोगि महेश्वर ।
सर्वपाप हरां देव मकाराय नमो नमः ॥

oṃ mahādeva mahātrāna mahāyogi maheśvara
sarvapāpa harāṃ deva makārāya namo namaḥ

Oṃ The Great God, the Great Reliever, the Great Yogi, Oh Supreme Lord, Oh God who removes all Sin, in the form of the letter “M” which dissolves creation, we bow to you again and again.

ॐ नमः शिवाय शान्ताय कारणत्राय हेतवे ।

निवेदायामि चात्मानं त्वं गति परमेश्वर ॥

oṃ namaḥ śivāya śāntāya kāraṇatrāya hetave
nivedāyāmi cātmānaṃ tvaṃ gati parameśvara

Oṃ I bow to the Consciousness of Infinite Goodness, to Peace, to the Cause of the three worlds, I offer to you the fullness of my soul, Oh Supreme Lord.

त्वमेव माता च पिता त्वमेव त्वमेव बन्धुश्च सखा त्वमेव ।

त्वमेव विद्या द्रविनं त्वमेव त्वमेव सर्वम् मम देवदेव ॥

tvameva mātā ca pitā tvameva
tvameva bandhuśca sakhā tvameva
tvameva vidyā dravinaṃ tvameva
tvameva sarvam mama deva deva

You alone are Mother and Father, you alone are friend and relative. You alone are knowledge and wealth, Oh my God of Gods, you alone are everything.

कयेन वच मनसेन्द्रियैर्व बुद्ध्यात्मा नव प्रकृत स्वभवत् ।

करोमि यद्यत् सकलम् परस्मै नारायणायेति समर्पयामि ॥

kayena vaca manasendriyairva
buddhyātmā nava prakṛta svabhavat
karomi yadyat sakalam parasmai
nārāyaṇāyeti samarpayāmi

Body, speech, mind, the five organs of knowledge (five senses) and the intellect; these nine are the natural condition of human existence. In their highest evolution, I move beyond them all, as I surrender completely to the Supreme Consciousness.

ॐ पापोऽहं पापकर्महं पापात्मा पापसम्भव ।

त्राहिमं पुण्डरीकक्षं सर्वपाप हरो हरि ॥

oṃ pāpo-haṃ pāpakarmahaṃ pāpātmā pāpasambhava trāhimaṃ puṇḍarīkakṣaṃ sarvapāpa haro hari

Oṃ I am of sin, confusion, duality; my actions are of duality; this entire existence is of duality. Oh Savior and Protector, Oh Great Consciousness, take away all sin, confusion, duality.

ॐ मन्त्रहीनं क्रियाहीनं भक्तिहीनं सुरेश्वरि ।

यत्पूजितं मया देवि परिपूर्णं तदस्तु मे ॥

oṃ mantrahīnaṃ kriyāhīnaṃ bhaktihīnaṃ sureśvari yatpūjitaṃ mayā devi paripūrnaṃ tadastu me

Oṃ I know nothing of mantras. I do not perform good conduct. I have no devotion, Oh Supreme Goddess. But Oh my Goddess, please accept the worship that I offer.

त्वमेव प्रत्यक्षम् ब्रह्माऽसि । त्वमेव प्रत्यक्षम् ब्रह्मा वदिश्यामि ।

रितम् वदिश्यामि, सत्यम् वदिश्यामि । तन मामवतु,

तद् वक्तारमवतु । अवतु माम्, अवतु वक्तारम् ॥

tvameva pratyakṣam brahmā-si tvameva pratyakṣam brahmā vadiśyāmi ritam vadiśyāmi, satyam vadiśyāmi tan māmavatu, tad vaktāramavatu avatu mām, avatu vaktāram

You alone are the Perceivable Supreme Divinity. You alone are the Perceivable Supreme Divinity, so I shall declare. I shall speak the nectar of immortality. I shall speak Truth. May this body be your instrument. May this mouth be your instrument. May the Divine always be with us. May it be thus.

ॐ सह नाववतु, सह नौ भुनक्तु । सह वीर्यं करवावहै ।

तेजस्विनावधीतमस्तु । मा विद्विशावहै ॥

oṃ saha nāvavatu saha nau bhunaktu
saha vīryam karavāvahai
tejasvināvadhītamastu mā vidviśāvahai

Oṃ May the Lord protect us. May the Lord grant us enjoyment of all actions. May we be granted strength to work together. May our studies be thorough and faithful. May all disagreement cease.

ॐ असतो मा सद्गमय । तमसो मा ज्योतिर्गमय ।

मृत्योर्मा अमृतं गमय ॥

oṃ asatomā sadgamaya
tamasomā jyotirgamaya
mṛtyormā amṛtaṃ gamaya

Oṃ From the untruth lead us to Truth. From darkness lead us to the Light. From death lead us to Immortality.

ॐ सर्वेषं स्वस्तिर्भवतु । सर्वेषं शान्तिर्भवतु ।

सर्वेषं पूर्णं भवतु । सर्वेषं मङ्गलं भवतु ।

सर्वे भवन्तु सुखिनः । सर्वे शन्तु निरमयाः ।

सर्वे भद्राणि पश्यन्तु । मा कश्चिद् दुःख भाग्भवेत् ॥

oṃ sarveṣaṃ svastir bhavatu
sarveṣaṃ śāntir bhavatu
sarveṣaṃ pūrṇaṃ bhavatu
sarveṣaṃ maṅgalaṃ bhavatu
sarve bhavantu sukhinaḥ sarve śantu niramayāḥ
sarve bhadrāṇi paśyantu
mā kaścid duḥkha bhāgbhavet

Gaṇeśa Pūjā

Oṃ May all be blessed with the highest realization. May all be blessed with Peace. May all be blessed with Perfection. May all be blessed with Welfare. May all be blessed with comfort and happiness. May all be free from misery. May all perceive auspiciousness. May all be free from infirmities.

गुरुर्ब्रह्मा गुरुर्विष्णुः गुरुर्देवो महेश्वरः ।
गुरुसाक्षात् परं ब्रह्मा तस्मै श्रीगुरवे नमः ॥

gurur brahmā gururviṣṇuḥ gururdevo maheśvaraḥ
gurusākṣāt paraṃ brahmā tasmai śrīgurave namaḥ

The Guru is Brahma, Guru is Viṣṇuḥ, Guru is the Lord Maheśvaraḥ. The Guru is actually the Supreme Divinity, and therefore we bow down to the Guru.

ॐ ब्रह्मार्पणं ब्रह्म हविर्ब्रह्माग्नौ ब्रह्मणा हुतम् ।
ब्रह्मैव तेन गन्तव्यं ब्रह्मकर्मसमाधिना ॥

oṃ brahmārpaṇaṃ brahma havir
brahmāgnau brahmaṇā hutam
brahmaiva tena gantavyaṃ brahmakarmasamādhinā

Oṃ The Supreme Divinity makes the offering; the Supreme Divinity is the offering; offered by the Supreme Divinity, in the fire of the Supreme Divinity. By seeing the Supreme Divinity in all actions, one realizes that Supreme Divinity.

ॐ पूर्णमदः पूर्णमिदं पूर्णात् पूर्णमुदच्यते ।
पूर्णस्य पूर्णमादाय पूर्णमेवावशिश्यते ॥

oṃ pūrṇamadaḥ pūrṇamidaṃ pūrṇāt pūrṇamudacyate
pūrṇasya pūrṇamādāya pūrṇamevāvaśiṣyate

Oṃ That is whole and perfect; this is whole and perfect. From the whole and perfect, the whole and perfect becomes manifest. If the whole and perfect issue forth from the whole and perfect, even still only the whole and perfect will remain.

ॐ शान्तिः शान्तिः शान्तिः

oṃ śāntiḥ śāntiḥ śāntiḥ

Oṃ Peace, Peace, Peace

अथ श्रीगणेश चालीसा

atha śrīgaṇeśa cālīsā

And now the Adventures of Gaṇeśa

दोहा

जय गणपति सद्गुण सदन कविवर बदन कृपाल ।

विघ्न हरण मंगल करण जय जय गिरिजालाल ॥

dohā

jaya gaṇapati sadguṇa sadana,
kavivara badana kṛpāla
vighna haraṇa maṃgala karaṇa,
jaya jaya girijālāla

Victory to the Lord of the Multitudes, who always exemplifies the qualities of purity, whose word is regarded as grace by inspired poets. He takes away all obstacles, is the cause of all welfare. Victory, victory to the son of the Daughter of the Mountain.

चौपाई

caupāī

जय जय जय गणपति गणराजू ।

मंगल भरण करण शुभ काजू ॥

jaya jaya jaya gaṇapati gaṇarājū
maṃgala bharaṇa karaṇa śubha kājū

Victory, Victory, Victory to the Lord of the Multitudes, King of the Multitudes, who grants welfare to all and is the cause of all pure actions.

जय गजवदन सदन सुख दाता ।
विश्व विनायक बुद्धि विधाता ॥

jaya gajavadana sadana sukha dātā
viśva vināyaka buddhi vidhātā

Victory to He with an elephant's head, who always grants comfort to all, who is the leader of the worlds and grantor of knowledge.

वक्र तुण्ड शुचि शुण्ड सुहावन ।
तिलक त्रिपुण्ड भाल मन भावन ॥

vakra tuṇḍa śuci śuṇḍa suhāvana
tilaka tripuṇḍa bhāla mana bhāvana

He has a bent tusk and radiates purity, on his forehead he wears the three marks of Śiva, which create the attitude of strength in the mind.

राजित मणि मुक्तन उर माला ।
स्वर्ण मुकुट शिर नयन विशाला ॥

rājita maṇi muktana ura mālā
svarṇa mukuṭa śira nayana viśālā

He wears a garland of gems and pearls, and on top of his head is a crown of gold. He has large eyes.

पुस्तक पाणि कुठार त्रिशूलं ।

मोदक भोग सुगन्धित फूलं ॥

pustaka pāṇi kuṭhāra triśūlaṃ
modaka bhoga sugandhita phūlaṃ

He has a book in his hand and a sharp trident. He enjoys sweets and fragrantly scented flowers.

सुन्दर पीताम्बर तन साजित ।

चरण पादुका मुनि मन राजित ॥

sundara pītāmbara tana sājita
caraṇa pādukā muni mana rājita

His body is clothed in a beautiful yellow cloth, and men of wisdom keep their minds fixed upon the wooden shoes on his feet.

धनि शिव सुवन षडानन भ्राता ।

गौरी ललन विश्व-विख्याता ॥

dhani śiva suvana ṣaḍānana bhrātā
gaurī lalana viśva-vikhyātā

He is the son of Śiva, brother of the one with six faces, the darling of Gauri, who is celebrated by the universe.

ऋद्धि सिद्धि तब चँवर सुधारे ।

मूषक वाहन सोहत द्वारे ॥

ṝddhi siddhi taba cam̐vara sudhāre
mūṣaka vāhana sohata dvāre

Prosperity and Attainment of Perfection fan him with yak's tails, he rides upon a mouse who stands at the door.

कहौं जन्म शुभ कथा तुम्हारी ।

अति शुचि पावन मंगल कारी ॥

kahauṃ janma śubha kathā tumhārī
ati śuci pāvana maṃgala kārī

It is said that the story of your birth is the cause of complete purity, emancipation and welfare.

एक समय गिरि राज कुमारी ।

पुत्र हेतु तप कीन्हा भारी ॥

eka samaya giri rāja kumārī
putra hetu tapa kīnhā bhārī

One time the Daughter of the King of the Mountains performed severe spiritual disciplines in order to have a child.

भयो यज्ञ जब पूर्ण अनृपा ।

तब पहुँच्यो तुम धरि द्विज रूपा ॥

bhayo yajña jaba pūrṇa anṛpā
taba pahuṁcyo tuma dhari dvija rūpā

Just when her sacrifice was full and complete, you arrived wearing the form of a twice born brahmin.

अथिति जानि कै गौरि सुखारी ।

बहु विधि सेवा करी तुम्हारी ॥

athiti jāni kai gauri sukhārī
bahu vidhi sevā karī tumhārī

Knowing you to be her guest, Gauri, She Who is Rays of Light, was greatly delighted, and in many ways she served you.

अति प्रसन्न ह्वै तुम वर दीन्ह ।

मातु, पुत्र हित जो तप कीन्हा ॥

ati prasanna hvai tuma vara dīnha
mātu, putra hita jo tapa kīnhā

Becoming very pleased you gave her the boon: Mother, whoever will perform this tapasya will become blessed with a child.

मिलहिं पुत्र तुहिं, बुद्धि विशाला ।

बिना गर्भ धारण, यहि काला ॥

milahiṃ putra tuhiṃ, buddhi viśālā
binā garbha dhāraṇa, yahi kālā

Now you will get a son with a tremendous intellect, without even becoming pregnant.

गणनायक, गुण, ज्ञान निधाना ।

पूजित प्रथम, रूप भगवाना ॥

gaṇanāyaka, guṇa, jñāna nidhānā
pūjita prathama, rūpa bhagavānā

He will be the Leader of the Multitudes, full of good qualities and wisdom, the form of God to be worshiped first.

अस कहि अन्तर्ध्यान रूप ह्वै ।

पलना पर बालक स्वरूप ह्वै ॥

asa kahi antardhyāna rūpa hvai
palanā para bālaka svarūpa hvai

Thus speaking his form dissolved within, and in a moment he assumed the form of a child.

बनि शिशु, रुदन जबहिं तुम ठानी ।

लखि मुख सुख नहिं गौरि समानी ॥

bani śiśu, rudana jabahiṃ tuma ṭhānī
lakhi mukha sukha nahiṃ gauri samānī

He became an infant child, and when his crying was heard, there was nothing to compare with the delight that was displayed on Gauri's face.

सकल मगन सुख मंगल गावहिं ।

नभ ते सुरन सुमन वर्षावहिं ॥

sakala magana sukha maṃgala gāvahiṃ
nabha te surana sumana varṣāvahiṃ

All sang songs intoxicated with delight, all exuded the greatest joy in singing praise and raining flowers.

शम्भु उमा, बहु दान लुटावहिं ।

सुर मुनिजन, सुत देखन आवहिं ॥

śambhu umā, bahu dāna luṭāvahiṃ
sura munijana, suta dekhana āvahiṃ

Śambhu and Umā gave many gifts, the Gods and the multitude of wise men came to see the divine child.

लखि अति आनन्द मंगल साजा ।

देखन भो, आये शनि राजा ॥

lakhi ati ānanda maṃgala sājā
dekhana bho, āye śani rājā

All could see that the divine child was blessed with great bliss and welfare. The King Saturn came.

निज अवगुण गुनि शनि मन माहीं ।

बालक, देखन चाहत नाहीं ॥

nija avaguṇa guni śani mana māhīṃ
bālaka, dekhana cāhata nāhīṃ

Saturn recognised the bad qualities in his own mind, and did not desire (or had hesitation) to see the divine child.

गिरिजा कुछ मन भेद बढायो ।

उत्सव मोर, न शनि तुहिं भायो ॥

girijā kucha mana bheda baḍhāyo
utsava mora, na śani tuhiṃ bhāyo

The Daughter of the Mountain expressed her mind, asking Saturn, "Do you disapprove of this festival?"

कहन लगे शनि, मन सकुचाई ।

का करिहो, शिशु मोहिं दिखाई ॥

kahana lage śani, mana sakucāī
kā kariho, śiśu mohiṃ dikhāī

She asked Saturn, whose mind was filled with desire, "Won't you see my child?"

नहिं विश्वास, उमा उर भयऊ ।

शनि सों बालक देखन कह्यऊ ॥

nahiṃ viśvāsa, umā ura bhayū
śani soṃ bālaka dekhana kahyaū

"I cannot believe, Uma, that he is yours," said Saturn when he saw the child.

पडतहिं शनि दृग कोण प्रकाशा ।

बालक शिर उडि गयो अकाशा ॥

paḍatahiṃ śani dṛga koṇa prakāśā
bālaka śira uḍi gayo akāśā

Saturn's light illuminated the farthest reaches in all directions, and the head of the child flew off into the heavens.

गिरिजा गिरो विकल ह्वै धरणी ।

सो दुख दशा गयो नहिं बरणी ॥

girijā giro vikala hvai dharaṇī
so dukha daśā gayo nahiṃ baraṇī

The Daughter of the Mountain fell to the ground, and she was in so much pain that it could not be any worse.

हाहाकार मच्यो कैलाशा ।

शनि कीन्ह्यो लखि सुत का नाशा ॥

hāhākāra macyo kailāśā
śani kīnhyo lakhi suta kā nāśā

Great sounds of distress permeated Kailaśa, because Saturn had slain the son of the Divine Mother.

तुरत गरुड चढि विष्णु सिधाये ।

काटि चक्र सों गजशिर लाये ॥

turata garuḍa caḍhi viṣṇu sidhāye
kāṭi cakra soṃ gajaśira lāye

Immediately Vishnu came flying on Garuḍa, and he cut the head of an elephant with his discus and brought it with him.

बालक के धड ऊपर धार्‌यो ।

प्राण, मन्त्र पडि शंकर डार्‌यो ॥

bālaka ke dhaḍa ūpara dhāryo
prāṇa, mantra paḍi śaṃkara ḍāryo

It was placed upon the torso of the child, and Śaṅkara recited the mantra which bestows life.

नाम गणेश शम्भु तब कीन्हें ।

प्रथम पूज्य बुधि निधि वर दीन्हें ॥

nāma gaṇeśa śambhu taba kīnheṃ
prathama pūjya budhi nidhi vara dīnheṃ

Then Śiva gave him the name Gaṇeśa and the boons of wisdom and of being first to be worshiped.

बुद्धि परीक्षा जब शिव कीन्हा ।

पृथ्वी कर प्रदक्षिण लीन्हा ॥

buddhi parīkṣā jaba śiva kīnhā
pṛthvī kara pradakṣiṇa līnhā

Śiva had a contest to see who would be the first to circumambulate the earth.

चले षडानन, भरमि भुलाई ।

रचे बेठि तुम बुद्धि उपाई ॥

cale ṣaḍānana, bharami bhulāī
race beṭhi tuma buddhi upāī

Kartikeya, the One with Six Heads, moved quickly, while Gaṇeśa, his brother, thought the matter over.

चरण मातु-पितु के धर लीन्हें ।

तिनके सात प्रदक्षिण कीन्हें ॥

caraṇa mātu-pitu ke dhara līnheṃ
tinake sāta pradakṣiṇa kīnheṃ

He bowed to the feet of his mother and father, and then he circumabulated them.

धनि गणेश कहि शिव हिय हर्ष्यो ।

नभ ते सुरन सुमन बहु बर्ष्यो ॥

dhani gaṇeśa kahi śiva hiya harṣyo
nabha te surana sumana bahu barṣyo

Śiva was very pleased with Gaṇeśa, and flowers fell in a rain from above.

तुम्हरी महिमा बुद्धि बडाई ।

शेष सहस मुख सके न गाई ॥

tumharī mahimā buddhi baḍāī
śeṣa sahasa mukha sake na gāī

The contemplation of your greatness expands intelligence, which Śeṣa Naga, the serphant of infinite energy with his thousand mouths, is unable to sing.

मैं मति हीन मलीन दुखारी ।

करहुँ कौन विधि विनय तुम्हारी ॥

maiṃ mati hīna malīna dukhārī
karahum̐ kaun vidhi vinaya tumhārī

I am extremely lowly, dirty and filled with pain, by which method can I humble myself before you?

भनत राम सुन्दर प्रभुदासा ।

लग प्रयाग ककरा दुर्वासा ॥

bhanata rāma sundara prabhudāsā
laga prayāga kakarā durvāsā

I am Rama Sundara Prabhudāsā, in the Kakarā Durvāsā section of the City of Prayāga, singing your praises.

अब प्रभु दया दीन पर कीजै ।

अपनो भक्ति शक्ति कछु दीजे ॥

aba prabhu dayā dona para kījai
apano bhakti śakti kachu dīje

Now, oh Lord, Giver of Compassion, give me more devotion and energy.

दोहा

dohā

श्री गणेश यह चालिसा, पाठ करै धरि ध्यान ।

नित नब मंगल गृह बसै, लहै जगत सनमान ॥

śrī gaṇeśa yaha cālisā, pāṭha karai dhari dhyān
nita naba maṃgala gṛha basai, lahai jagata sanamāna

This is the song known as The Adventures of Gaṇeśa. Whoever will recite these forty verses with attention will eternally reside in the house of welfare and become the recipient of respect in this world.

सम्बत अयन सहस्र दश, ऋषि पञ्चमी दिनेश ।

पूरण चालीसा भयो, मंगल मूर्ति गणेश ॥

sambata ayana sahasra daśa, ṛṣi pañcamī dineśa
pūraṇa cālīsā bhayo, maṃgala mūrti gaṇeśa

Gaṇeśa Pūjā

In the Saṃskṛt year 1010, on the fifth day of the ṛṣis, these ancient forty verses have been recited in praise of Gaṇeśa, the image of welfare.

In Tantra Philosophy there are thirty-six principles. They begin with Sadāśiva and Śakti; these are two separate principles, but they are united as One. Sadāśiva is Pure Consciousness, while Śakti is Pure Energy. Iśvara is the principle of union between Śiva and Śakti, Ardanārīśvara, both male and female. Then comes Śuddha Vidyā, pure know- ledge. You have seen the picture of Śiva with his eyes just barely starting to open, when Śiva says, "I have a feeling that there is something else out there other than me." Māyā is the next principle. "She is different from me. I am Śiva and there She is, the Divine Mother, the measurement or limitation of consciousness." Māyā is perceived through five kāñchūkas, limitations, or modes of perception. They are kāla - time, nyāti - space, rāga - activity, being or becoming, vidyā - knowledge of name and form, and kalā - attributes. These five kāñchūkas make ten principles in descending order. Then comes Puruṣa, the individual soul or consciousness, and Prakṛti, the embodiment of nature.

Ahaṃkāra is the ego, the sense of I. Citta is the totality of all cognition comprised of buddhi and manas. Buddhi means objective knowledge, or what is, in other words all of the nouns and verbs of experience. Manas, on the other hand, is subjective knowledge, or what we think about things. Manas comprises the adjectives and adverbs. Buddhi says this is a book. Manas says this is a good book. The good is the interpretation of manas. Both together are citta, objective and subjective experience, the world as it is and the world as we think it to be, our relationship to it. These four together: ahaṃkāra, citta, buddhi and manas, are called the antaḥkaraṇa, the inner cause or inner sense.

Then there are twenty principles which define the gross world and our relationship to it. Five of these principles are called tanmātras, which are the objects of perception: sight, sound, smell, taste and feel. Five are called mahābhūtas, which are the essential elements of existence: earth, water, fire, air and ether. Then there are five organs of know-ledge: the eyes, ears, nose, tongue and skin, jñān-endriyas. Then there are the five organs of action, karmendriyas, which are the upper appendages, lower appendages, the tongue, reproductive organs, and anus.

These principles disclose how divinity descended into manifested existence. In order to go back to the origin, we must come and go by the same path. We begin by controlling the organs of action, because they are the ones that interact with the outside world. We put our body into such a harmony so as to control the organs of knowledge. Close the nine doors to the City of God. Control the karm-endriyas -- the organs of action and the jñān-endriyas -- the organs of knowledge. We recognize the five elements of existence and their five objects of perception in the subtle body: earth, water, fire, air, ether; sight, sound, smell, taste, and feeling. Let your energy climb the cakras, and put the twenty principles into the balance of harmony.

Now put manas, buddhi, citta, into balance. Control the ego, ahaṃkāra. This is the twenty-fourth principle. This is the body of Prakṛti, the body of Nature expressed through the individual, perceived by Puruṣa, which is twenty-sixth. This Puruṣa has been perceived in time, space, activity, knowledge, and with attributes. By moving beyond these modes of perception, which constitute thirty-one principles, we move into māyā. Then we see Śiva in Śuddha Vidyā, faintly aware that there is another outside. Let him close his eyes. Īśvara is next, then Śakti and Sadāśiva. These are the thirty-six principles, which are the path to absorption in the unmanifest.

Every being manifested and every moment that comes to birth, comes to birth because of our unfinished business. There is some reason that it comes into manifestation, and the arrows we have shot will land. When the stimulus does come, do we react reflexively, or do we control ourselves and design a response that will bring us closer to what we want in the furtherance of our goals? Do we know what we want? Or do we react emotionally on transient impulses? When we react emotionally, are we not creating more karma for ourselves, so that once again we condemn ourselves to wait for those new arrows to land?

It is evident that the difference between the yogī, the being of union, and the bhogī, the being of selfish enjoyment, is that moment of discrimination which is the interlude between stimulus and response. There is a moment of recollection, a moment of remembrance, in which the yogī asks, "What do I want to attain from these circumstances?" Before I respond emotionally and get my ego involved in what I perceive to be a stimulus, before I even calculate the appropriate response, I must ask myself, "What do I want to get?" Only when I know what my objective is, can I possibly consider the next question, "What action of mine would bring me closer to that goal?"

There are four kinds of karma in existence. Saṃkṣipta is the karma which is completed, over and done with. It is finished. It is full, complete, and perfect. There is nothing more left to be done. Vartmāna is present karma, that karma which is going on right now. It is in process. Prārabdha karma are the actions which were begun in the past and which will come to fruition in the future.

Śaṅkarācārya uses the analogy of the arrow which leaves the bow of the archer. Once the arrow has set forth from the bow, there is nothing that the archer can do to alter its course, but to watch and see where it may land. He has no control after it has left the bow. This is what we call prārabdha karma. Every action is an arrow that has already been released. All of us are the actors, waiting for our arrows to land. When an arrow lands, if we react, we shoot another arrow. The arrows continue in rapid succession until we cultivate the spirit of renunciation known as udāsa. U means circumstance. Dāsa means the servant of. Udāsa literally and philologically means the servant of circumstances. It symbolizes acceptance, freedom from reaction, complete surrender. When one attains udāsa, the spirit of surrendering, then there is total acceptance of ever circumstance without the shooting of new arrows. We free ourselves from the reactions of desire or revulsion. We see all of the prārabdha karma that commenced in the past and watch dispassionately as all of those arrows land, without firing again.

The fourth kind of karma is known as nityakarma, eternal karma. Nityakarma actually means yoga. It is complete union. Yoga is defined as citta vṛtti nirodha. Citta means the objects of awareness, the objects of consciousness. Vṛtti means activities or modifications. Nirodha means prohibition, cessation, or obstruction. When there is a complete cessation of the activities of the objects of consciousness, there is a perfectly still consciousness. When there is no modification or change, there is yoga, union. Yoga is nityakarma, eternal; the activities which are eternal. Citta vṛtti nirodha is the perfect stillness of consciousness, without activities, modifications or changes in awareness.

Traditionally there are four aspects of yoga: dhyāna - meditation, jñāna - wisdom, bhakti - devotion, and karma - activity. These four are inseparably connected, but spoken of as four different disciplines so that seekers can intellectually understand the distinctions between them. However, in reality, without devotion how can we pay attention? Without knowledge how can we perform effective action? Without effective action how can we gain knowledge? Thus the four aspects of yoga are inseparably connected in the path of union, and are not different disciplines, but actually are the four components of one path.

From the moment of conception in the womb, the life of duality begins. That first awareness of individuality comes as a result of prārabdha karma. We have a lot of outstanding debts. We have many arrows that have been shot off into the atmosphere, and we are waiting for them to land. That is prārabdha karma. It is for the purpose of perfecting that karma, of fulfilling the destiny that we ourselves have created, that we have all taken birth. And then every moment of our lives takes birth as a consequence of the same prārabdhavaśāt janma. So every birth takes place because of prārabdha karma - the birth of every moment in time, the birth of every circumstance, and the birth of every being. It all takes place in the fulfillment of the process of karma, prārabdhavaśāt janma.

All birth takes place in order to finish karma: the birth of every reaction, the birth of every relationship, the birth of every moment, the birth of everybody. That is our function, our purpose. We are all bound by unfinished karma. With this knowledge it behooves us to perform every action as thoroughly and efficiently as possible, so we don't have to come back to finish our incomplete work. Bound by unfinished karma is birth, which is the birth of every action, every moment.

To attain freedom from reaction, we must remember that the prārabdha karma is the arrow that is coming to land. When it lands and hits its mark, then we react and send off another arrow. If only we could stop and look where it landed before we start shooting off arrows again. If we must respond, we should give a response designed to free ourselves from further troubles. We should think about what we are going to do. Such discrimination would mean living life perfectly. Our responses should be calculated to take us to a better place than we are already at, responses designed to accomplish our objectives. If we could just find some way to ask ourselves, "What do I want to accomplish before I react? What do I want to get before I respond to this? What would be an appropriate response designed to get what I want?" If we could just stop and put one instant of discrimination between the stimulus and the response, then we could live life perfectly.

There are traditionally eight limbs of yoga. The first one is called yāma, to take control. One takes control in life by defining goals. It is not possible to find a path until we know what the goal is. Without this knowledge we cannot prevent ourselves from moving in the direction of any other force greater than our own. So we must begin the process of union with a clear definition of the goal.

The second step in yoga is called niyama, which means to create a discipline. We must budget our time, budget our resources, and budget our mind. How much can we dedicate in the pursuit of each of our goals? Without a clear definition of our goals and the discipline with which to attain them, it is impossible to have criteria with which to discriminate which actions will take us closer, and which will actually take us farther away. Without criteria for discrimination, all actions become extremely arbitrary. We find no capacity to devote ourselves to the higher disciplines of putting our bodies, our breath, our senses, and ultimately, our minds into harmony.

The third step of yoga is called āsana, putting the body in harmony. Āsana literally means to sit quietly and to make one's self present. It does not necessary mean to twist yourself up like a pretzel. More often it refers to the practice of putting your body into such a state of harmony and balance that you no longer require to pay attention to it. The body in balance is free from need. Therefore, it sits quietly, allowing one to make one's self present. The primary reason for practicing various hātha yoga postures is to train the body to sit still.

The fourth step of yoga is called prāṇāyāma, controlling the breath. The breath is a vehicle by which we rejuvenate the body, and a vehicle out of control is extremely dangerous. By paying attention to the breath, we regulate the length of each cycle of inhalation, retention and exhalation, and maintain vigilance over the qualities that are energizing our systems. There are several formulas for prāṇāyāma depending upon the purpose. We will discuss some of the more classical means of controlling breath in greater detail later.

The fifth step of yoga is called pratyāhāra, withdrawing of the senses from the objects of sense. It means to bring your senses inside. Stop looking outside, close all of your senses. Look within.

Then comes dhāraṇā, concentration. Collect all of the different thoughts in the mind and concentrate on one of them. In dhāraṇā there are three: subject, object and relationship. "I love you." There is a lover, a recipient of the love, and the love which binds us together.

In dhyāna, meditation, the next step in the path to union, there are only two: subject and object. The relationship is understood. In meditation there is an undefinable intuitive cognition. It is often curious to listen to people speak of meditation practices before they have organized their lives or defined their goals or established their discipline. Most probably there is a confusion between introspection, day-dreaming and meditation. Undoubtedly the practice and the attainment are described by the same word, but dhyāna as it applies to the path of yoga refers to absorption in meditation.

Samādhi means completion, accomplishment, the perfection of union. In samādhi there is only One.

There are three general areas of samādhi. The first is called bhāva samādhi. This is an intensity of awareness, an attitude. In bhāva three things exist: subject ahaṃ, object tvaṃ, and their relationship, for example, "I am your devotee" or "I love you." There are two types of this samādhi described in Saṃskṛt literature. The first is sālokya. Loka means world. In our usage it means a paradigm of reality. Sa means with or in the same world: in immediate proximity to each other, in the same paradigm of reality and togetherness. It can be physical or metaphysical, but there is a togetherness. We are in this plane of reality together.

The second is called sāmipya. We are performing the same karma. Just as you are doing, so I am also doing. I see you sitting there doing prāṇāyāma, breathing love into the entire universe, and I am sitting here performing the same prāṇāyāma, making jāpa of the same mantra, breathing the same love into the universe. You and I are one in the performance of the same activity. These are the two forms of bhāva samādhi.

The second kind of samādhi is called savikalpa, with an idea. Vikalpa means an idea and sa means with. Savikalpa has two types of samādhi. Sarūpa means with form. I have an idea that your form and my form are alike. I look at you and it is like looking in the mirror. You and I have the same form. I have an idea of ahaṃ - tvaṃ, but the relationship is understood. In the bhāva there are three things: subject, object and the union between them, their relationship. In savikalpa there are only two things, subject and object. There is a prakāśa. The relationship is not intellectual. Intuitively, I see sarūpa. I am looking in the mirror. I see you, my deity, my perfect reflection.

Sadṛṣṭi means with perception. Just as I am perceiving you, so you are perceiving me. Which one is the reality, and which one is the reflection? Who can say? There is no one else. There is no other relationship by which to define.

The third type of samādhi is called nirvikalpa. Nir means without - without an idea. There is only one form of nirvikalpa samādhi called sayuja. Yuja means union. Sa means with. The perfection of union. That is the Vedic sayings, "Ahaṃ Brahmāsmi" or "tat tvaṃ asi." It is all ahaṃ or it is all tvaṃ. But there is no other option.

Bhāva, savikalpa, nirvikalpa. Sālokya, sāmipya, sarūpa, sadṛṣṭi, sayuja. These are the different forms of prakāśa. Sālokya is in the same paradigm of reality. Sāmipya is in the same activity. Sarūpa is having the same appearance. Sadṛṣṭi is having the same perception. Sayuja is we are the same. These are the five kinds of prakāśa experienced in meditation.

We begin our journey inwards from the annamaya kośa, the world of aṇu or atoms, that which is perceivable through the senses. The prāṇamaya kośa is the world of breath. The breath is the relationship between the outer world and the inner world. It is the avenue by which we bring oxygen from the outside in and put carbon dioxide from the inside out. From the prāṇamaya kośa we move to manomaya kośa; the world of concepts, ideas, thoughts. From the manomaya kośa we move to the vijñānamaya kośa, the world of light, the light of wisdom; all thoughts merging into the light of wisdom. From the vijñānamaya kośa we take all the light of wisdom and merge it into the ānandamaya kośa, sat cit ānanda, truth, infinite consciousness and pure bliss.

Remember the path by which we come is the means by which we return. From the ānandamaya kośa, we move into the vijñānamaya kośa; take all the bliss and put it into the light of wisdom. From the vijñānamaya kośa we move into the manomaya kośa, and take the light of wisdom and illuminate all of thought. Fill your thoughts with love, joy and beauty. Take all of those thoughts from the manomaya kośa and put them into the prāṇamaya kośa, and exhale love, joy, wisdom and peace into the creation.

These are the pañca kośa, the five sheaths, coverings or layers, in order from their most gross to their more subtle forms. These are the avenues by which we bring our awareness from the outside world to the inside. Prāṇa is an avenue of ingress and egress, bringing our awareness inside by following the breath.

Gaṇeśa is the Lord of Wisdom and He won the boon that He would be the first one worshipped in any rite of spiritual passage. Pūjā is the nitya karma which allows us to retrace the steps from manifested existence and to return to the unmanifest. It is true that without wisdom it will be impossible for any seeker to unlock the doors to the secrets of enlightenment. Gaṇeśa grants that boon. May He be pleased with our efforts and bless us all with the highest attainment.

Books by Shree Maa and Swami Satyananda Saraswati

Annapūrṇa Thousand Names
Before Becoming This
Bhagavad Gītā
Chaṇḍi Pāṭh
Cosmic Pūjā
Cosmic Pūjā Bengali
Devī Gītā
Devī Mandir Songbook
Durgā Pūjā Beginner
Ganeśa Pūjā
Gems From the Chaṇḍi
Guru Gītā
Hanumān Pūjā
Kālī Dhyānam
Kālī Pūjā
Lakṣmī Sahasra Nāma
Lalitā Triśati
Sahib Sadhu
Shree Maa - The Guru & the Goddess
Shree Maa, The Life of a Saint
Śiva Pūjā Beginner
Śiva Pūjā and Advanced Fire Ceremony
Sundara Kāṇḍa
Swāmī Purāṇa

Gaṇeśa Pūjā

Cassette Tapes and CDs by Shree Maa

Chaṇḍi Pāṭh

Lalitā Triśati

Navarṇa Mantra

Oh Dark Night Mother

Sādhu Stories from the Himalayas

Shree Maa at the Devi Mandir

Shree Maa in Mendocino

Shree Maa in the Temple of the Heart

Shiva is in My Heart

Śiva Pūjā Beginner

Śiva Pūjā and Advanced Fire Ceremony

The Goddess is Everywhere

The Songs of Ramprasad

The Thousand Names of Kālī

Please visit us on the World Wide Web at http://www.shreemaa.org email: info@shreemaa.org

www.ingramcontent.com/pod-product-compliance
Ingram Content Group Australia Pty Ltd
76 Discovery Rd, Dandenong South VIC 3175, AU
AUHW021316290425
410369AU00003B/35

9 781877 795466